Making Change Stick

Twelve Principles for
Transforming Organizations

Richard C. Reale

 Positive Impact Associates, Inc.

ISBN 0-976-85010-9

Library of Congress Control Number: 2005905166

First edition: August 2005
Second printing: November 2006
Third printing: July 2009
Fourth printing: December 2010

Published by Positive Impact Associates, Inc.

For additional copies of this book, please visit
www.p-impact.com

Printed in the U.S.A. by
Signature Book Printing, Inc.

Contents

Figures

Preface

FOR the last twenty years I have been studying why programs fail and why change refuses to stick. Organizational change often breaks down because of failure to consider the human side of change.

Listen up, all you task-focused problem solvers! Getting the soft stuff right is in fact the hard part. Most organizations know what they need to do. They have the skills and technology. They just can't bring it all to bear on the problem to effect a lasting change.

People laugh at the cliché about consultants reading your watch to tell you what time it is, but there is a nugget of truth in it. While knowing the correct time is important, it does not guarantee prompt arrival at our destination. Knowing what needs to change does not ensure the ability to propagate the change and make it stick.

Making change stick is about having the right process. Many leaders have gravitated to the technical side of change and have all but ignored the human side. The principles in this book are a guide for creating a *change-capable* organization. They form a blueprint for developing a human process that can assimilate change effectively. An organization's people make or break change. **Focus on the people and you empower them to focus on the change**.

When I ask leaders if their organization has trouble coming up with great ideas, the answer is a resounding "No". But the response changes when we discuss the organization's ability to implement those ideas. The problem clearly is not brain power but something related to individual motivation during the *doing* part.

If you want to understand the issues, walk a mile in the shoes of people who have to implement a change they didn't ask for and had no voice in. Imagine how you would feel if you arrived at work to learn that the world of work, as you understand it, was coming to an end.

The principles discussed in this book follow basic human nature and allow change to take root in the gardens of those who till the soil. When the principles are followed, people can respond to change as willing collaborators rather than as victims.

Stick with it!

> *It's not the strongest or the most intelligent that survive, but rather the most adaptable.*
> ~ *Charles Darwin*

Introduction

Why Change Doesn't Always Stick

*There is nothing more difficult to take in hand, more
perilous to conduct, or more uncertain in its success than
to take the lead in the introduction of a new order of
things.*   ~ *Niccolo Machiavelli*

SISYPHUS puts his back into rolling the monstrous stone
up the hill, grunting and sweating as he inches his
way toward the top. And then it happens—the stone
overpowers him and tumbles back down the hill,
beckoning him to repeat the process.

Have you ever tried to change something only to find
that over time the change seems to evaporate, leaving
you exactly where you started? Most of us have had this
experience many times. It happens in our organizations
as well.

Today's turbulent marketplace leaves hardly a
niche untouched by mandatory "change or die"
imperatives. Business prognosticators suggest that
both the frequency and amount of change required
will escalate over the next few decades. Our survival
requires that we become more resilient and more
effective at making change stick.

Survival isn't achieved by standing still; of the top one
hundred companies in 1900, fewer than 20 percent are
still in business. Just as fire is essential to the long-term

health of our forests, ongoing systemic change and reinvention are critical to organizational survival.

The key question is, why does change so often fail to stick? On closer examination perhaps it's not that we regressed but rather that the change was more illusion than reality. We painted a few eggs gold in the expectation that the goose would be inspired, get the picture, and start laying golden ones. The elements necessary to accomplish and sustain the change were neither identified nor implemented.

When change is sticky, outcomes are not facades but predictable outputs of a physical, mental, and emotional process. **Sticky change takes commitment**. Sticky change takes place at the systemic level.

Sticky change frequently requires the adaptation of culture. Culture can be described as a set of shared attitudes, values, and behavioral patterns. Long-term survival and outstanding performance depend on being a culturally open system, ready to adapt as necessary to prosper under any market conditions.

Business has become like catching a connecting flight in an unfamiliar airport with only a few minutes between a late arrival and your next scheduled departure. Since the market is a moving target, there is no gold standard for a corporate culture other than being dynamically adaptive and supportive of the needs of customers, employees, and shareholders.

While the market has become a moving target, the process of human change has not. After many years of observing both successful and unsuccessful changes in a variety of organizations, I have discerned a series of repeating patterns and distilled them into the twelve principles described in this book. Change-capable organizations adhere to these principles. When change doesn't stick, invariably one or more of the twelve principles has been ignored or violated.

<u>**Principles for Making Change Stick**</u>

1. Know where you are going

2. Challenge your thinking

3. Involve and be involved

4. Align your culture

5. Honor emotions

6. Confront fear

7. Don't wait for perfection

8. Communicate intentionally

9. Set people up for success

10. Catch people doing something right

11. Measure stuff that matters

12. Lead from the heart

Figure 1. Principles for Making Change Stick

These principles provide a roadmap for improving any organization's ability to adapt, which is paramount to long-term survival and prosperity. We **make change stick** when we can dynamically adapt to and sustain the change until the next challenge or opportunity arrives.

The twelve principles of making change stick provide us with a way to create a well-marked trail to help individuals find their way through the dense forest of change. There are many unmarked paths and forks within the forest. Without clear trail markings it's easy to become disoriented and lose our way. A trail map and clear markings make it easier to understand where each fork leads and how to stay on the path that leads to the meeting point on the other side of the forest.

While it is leadership's job to scout the forest and mark the trail, we may not see all the possible forks in the path. Just getting through the forest is not the same thing as seeing the forest through the eyes of those who will follow. The twelve principles help us see the hidden tricky spots along the trail and appropriately mark and map them so that others can more easily choose the best path to the rendezvous.

Meticulously followed, the twelve principles for making change stick put the responsibility for change squarely on the shoulders of every person in the organization. The twelve principles put all participants—leaders and followers—in charge of leading themselves. To change is to choose: victim or collaborator, the choice is ours.

1 Know Where You Are Going

*You got to be careful if you don't know
where you're going, because you might not
get there.*

~ *Yogi Berra*

Sticky change requires clarity both in **where** the organization needs to go and **why.** Reasons for change should be purposeful and strategically important. If you have a vision and mission statement for your organization, this is a good time to take it out, dust it off, and see whether it's still relevant to current conditions. Unfortunately, most organizations' documented visions become stagnant rather than remaining living maps pointing to the future.

In and of themselves, vision and mission statements don't accomplish much. I am an advocate of the visioning process but not preoccupied with the perfection of the end product. I have learned that the real magic occurs during the journey of introspection and creation. The final written document is much less important than the process by which it is created.

Written statements prepared by an individual or small group usually miss the mark. A vision of the future is more importantly in the hearts and minds of those aspiring to the new place than on some stone tablet chiseled by the few.

I've had leaders swear to me that their organizations didn't have a vision or mission statement, later to find an attractively framed one hanging on the wall between the elevators! The point is that writing it down doesn't make it so, only living and sharing it does. Most people will not subscribe to someone else's vision without an experience that connects it with their own.

Your statements must provide a clear image of what the successful post-change future looks like. **If you can see it, then you can be it**. The clearer and more detailed the description of the new state, the better.

A key component is to describe not only the physical manifestations of the change but also the behavioral ones. What mind-set is needed to achieve the new level of performance necessary for success? A question of this type opens the door to underlying values and worldviews that need to be discussed—and possibly reframed—to achieve an organizational change that will stick.

Involve as many members of the organization as possible as you look forward. Collect everyone's ideas and descriptions of the post-change organization. Creating a shared vision of the change will provide a deeper understanding of and commitment to the future organization.

Values Count

Experience has taught me that values have a significant impact on the way an organization thinks and performs. The good news is that closely held core values rarely have to change, although our interpretation of them sometimes does. For example, hard work is measured in one organization with a clock, in another by tangible results. The different interpretations of the same core value produce dramatically different results in each organization. Long hours at work may not produce the needed results and sometimes even prevent them.

> *You never have to change what you see, only the way you see it.* ~ *Thaddeus Golas*

I have facilitated processes designed to envision the future with as few as three and as many as several thousand people. Regardless of group size, it is essential to clarify values and adopt a common definition of the way the organization must be. Open dialogue is needed for participants to understand and internalize changes.

I've found that few management teams are on the same page regarding their values, despite what they say. Some organizations fear opening the Pandora's box of values, but in any systemic change value or interpretation differences arise whether they are addressed explicitly or not. It is better to navigate the difficult hurdles when designing the change than to be derailed by unanticipated difficulties during implementation.

Once the future state is clarified, communicate with everyone in the organization. This communication is not a laminated card or a notice in the company newsletter; communication of key strategic information must be bi-directional, soliciting the thoughts and feelings of everyone affected by the change. When the process is complete, everyone should be clear on where the organization must go and how the change will be created and sustained.

On The Same Page

A small manufacturing company had received a grant for management training. I provided communication, team building, problem solving, and change management training to senior management and their direct reports. The company was family-owned, with the founder's son and his three sons directly involved in the business.

It became clear during the training that many managers were frustrated with the organization's inability to change; the rest of the management team was utterly confused about where the company was headed. I passed my observations on to the president, recommending a strategic planning session to bring some clarity. The president agreed, although not optimistically; their previous attempts had ended with little improvement.

Prior to the retreat I performed a behavioral and values assessment of every participant and graphed their results as a group. I discovered that the owners, who displayed an introverted, relationship-oriented style, were dramatically different from the balance of the leadership team.

Interested in growing the company, they had hired people with strong experience who had demonstrated results in other organizations.

These new managers were outgoing, assertive, confrontational, and quick to act. The owners were uncomfortable with the new leaders' rapid pace and "in your face" style. The newcomers were pressing to move forward rapidly while the owners, out of concern, were delaying the process.

Failure to understand behavioral differences naturally led to misattributions of meaning. Concerns about individual commitment, competency, and caring were triggered by each group's "strange" behaviors. Conflict escalated within senior management, leaving the rest of the organization in confusion.

The retreat began with discussion of the behavioral differences on the management team, how those differences could be strengths for the organization, and under what conditions they could lead to derailment. We followed with a dialogue about values and a review of the company's vision and mission statements.

It was amazing to feel the shift in energy in the room as the session progressed. With behavioral differences openly discussed and better understood, a door opened to unexpected points of agreement and new opportunities born of diversity. A fundamental change occurred in the group's cohesiveness that allowed them to reach a common understanding regarding direction. Able to agree both intellectually and emotionally about necessary changes to their company, they transcended conflict to find synergy.

I believe this progress was made because the process created an opportunity for the owners to see and believe that the rest of the team, despite their different behaviors, shared their core values and desires for the future of the company. They were even able to agree that the public name and identity of the company should be changed to transmit their strategic intention more clearly to their customers.

Questions To Ponder

? Why do we exist as an organization? What purpose do we fulfill?

? How will the change we are undertaking take us closer to our vision?

? How are my daily actions connected to the organization's mission?

? How could I modify my daily actions to be more in line with the organization's purpose?

? Can I explain to others how their actions are directly related to the mission of the organization?

? If I asked people what the organization was trying to achieve, would they be able to answer? How would they answer?

? Where do I think the organization will be in three years? In ten years? What do I want my role to be?

Putting The Principle Into Practice

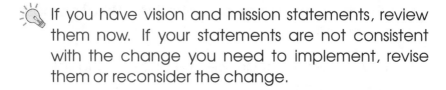 If you have vision and mission statements, review them now. If your statements are not consistent with the change you need to implement, revise them or reconsider the change.

If you don't have vision and mission statements, consider putting effort into developing them. Involve as many people as possible in the creation of your organizational vision and mission.

Document the core values of your organization and how they are demonstrated.

Identify high-performing individuals in your organization and try to pinpoint the values they exhibit through their desirable behaviors. These are likely to be the core values of the organization.

Identify the behavioral styles and values of the leadership team and discuss how similarities and differences affect group and organizational cohesiveness.

Develop a detailed "what would it look like?" description of the post-change organization.

Engage people by exploring organizational values and direction rather than by telling.

Challenge Your Thinking

*Congealed thinking is the forerunner of
failure… make sure you are always receptive
to new ideas.*

~ George Crane

As human beings we possess the capacity for meta-cognition, which is simply the ability to think about how we think. Challenging our thinking—especially in the context of organizational change—includes being aware of our mental models: how they are formed, how they affect us, and how we can change them.

How we view and understand the world is based on our own unique mental constructs. Since reality is extremely complex and our senses are limited, our mental models exhibit varying degrees of accuracy. Being able to construct workable models quickly is helpful in negotiating our everyday lives. Imagine a caveman stuck in analysis paralysis trying to perfect his mental model in the path of a charging Mastodon.

While making models quickly is a useful survival skill, we create problems for ourselves when we confuse our models with reality. Alfred Korzybski, a semanticist, reminds us of this hazard in his saying, "The map is not the territory." Maps are never 100% true to the detail of reality but they are usually adequate for finding our way. We constantly build upon, combine, and refine our mental models as we have new experiences, but the models will never be identical to reality.

Comparing current sensory input to similar stored patterns forges new models from old ones. Language, through the use of metaphors, helps expedite the process of linking to existing models. New variants of existing models can be created through analogy, like learning how electrons flow in a wire by understanding how water flows in a pipe. Language is incredibly powerful because it helps the brain conduct this natural process of comparison, linkage, and construction.

Models are built upon each other like a pyramid of oranges stacked up at the supermarket. It's not a big deal to change an orange at the top of the pyramid, but tension escalates when one of the oranges on the bottom smells a little funny. It's scary to imagine that whole mountain of oranges collapsing. The more contrary a new idea appears to conventional wisdom (existing models), the deeper into the pile one must go to resolve the disparity. People are often so afraid of unraveling their belief systems that any suggestion of inaccuracy in their models evokes instant resistance.

If you have to sell a new idea that sounds like heresy, take time to develop an honest rationale that explains the apparent contradiction. In his book *Quality Is Free* [1], Philip Crosby developed such a rationale to explain why high-quality products don't have to cost more than low-quality products, thereby debunking that piece of conventional wisdom.

The Impossible Takes A Little Longer

> *The significant problems we face today cannot be solved at the same level of thinking we were at when we created them.* ~ *Albert Einstein*

When we face large systemic change, we may think that we have failed in not recognizing what had to happen or that our current ways are wrong. Einstein captured the essence of the matter, realizing that we can solve problems only up to our level of understanding at the time we address them. This is not a disparagement of our previous work but a recognition that knowledge increases over time. Most likely the current system was a breakthrough idea from an older system.

We might imagine being on an elevator and exploring a building floor by floor. Every time we are lifted up to a new floor there unfolds an entirely new landscape full of items we have never seen before. Some things even appear impossible. How do we go about understanding what we are seeing?

When we declare that something is impossible, we base our judgment on the models we have used before. If the models contradict what we are seeing, we may even discount the evidence of our senses. The more successful our models have been in the past, the more likely we are to deny the validity of what we are seeing.

The changes that are needed in most organizations today are more like that elevator ride to the next floor than finding another room to explore on our current floor. There has been much comparison made in business to the paradigm shift that occurred in physics when quantum theory was first proposed. I believe there are worthwhile metaphors in that comparison and lessons to be learned from the disturbed scientists who had the security blanket of Newtonian physics ripped from their hands.

> *If the facts don't fit the theory, change the facts.*
> *~ Albert Einstein*

Looking to the next level of thinking is a transition in itself. It requires us to let go of the comfort we have with our existing models. We may need to deconstruct what we know and reassemble it into a new reality. One important idea that had its birth in science is the concept of "both/and". Scientists call this *wave-particle duality*. It means that photons act as both waves and particles depending on what the scientist is looking for.

Those of us in business can draw a parallel when we realize that many things we deal with are based on an either/or model. For years price and quality were thought to have an either/or relationship. The expression, "You get what you pay for" (or, as I say, "You don't get what you don't pay for") reflects this model. Either you pay for quality or you get junk. The quality revolution of the last two decades has changed things so that one can now expect both good quality and a good price.

Think Outside The Box

It is likely that either/or models will crop up when we attempt to implement systemic change. Categorical statements such as, "We can't do it" or "It's not possible" are often based on either/or thinking. To help break the mental logjam and open the door to both/and thinking, try modifying such statements by adding a qualifying phrase: "the way we do it now". Then follow up with questions like, "Under what conditions would this be possible?"

Carefully crafted questions open the door to outside-the-box thinking. The imagination transcends rigid barriers. Interestingly, as children we called it *make believe*. Those two words cemented together give us the permission and the power to create possibilities beyond present reality.

Sometimes our thinking gets stuck and it becomes difficult to shift direction and adapt to changes that challenge the status quo. Over time, underlying models that have not been challenged tend to solidify into fixed beliefs. They move from being concepts into the groove of "truth".

Making changes usually requires modifying something that we believe. While this may sound ominous, we typically modify scores of beliefs every day without incident. It's easy because the beliefs in question are usually inconsequential. We may have beliefs about the products we use or ways to do mundane things or perhaps who makes the best pizza in town. The more personal a belief becomes, however, the stronger it is and the more difficult to modify.

Our most strongly held beliefs are those connected to our identity. Perhaps that's why title changes can have such a large impact on people. Be it Chief Engineer or best typist in the office, people have a tendency to equate their intrinsic worth with what they do or what they have accomplished. Changes that challenge beliefs about our identity or beliefs formed through significant personal experiences often cause our castle drawbridge to rise. Our ability to solve problems greatly diminishes as our defenses become impenetrable even to our own reflective inquiry.

 I've begun calling beliefs *frozen assumptions* in an effort to remind myself that behind each of these beliefs is a series of assumptions. My experience has been that uncovering a faulty assumption in my thinking is much less traumatic than admitting to a faulty belief!

As we continue to think about unresolved problems we may feel as though nothing is happening, but in reality subtle shifts in thinking are continuous. I've been mystified at times as answers to unsolved problems suddenly pop into my head when I'm thinking about something else. I believe that questioning our assumptions can accelerate this process.

> *You must stick to your conviction, but be ready to abandon your assumptions.* ~ Denis Waitley

First, Assume That You Assume...

Just as an engineer solving a problem must justify the assumption that some forces are negligible, we must also scrutinize the validity of our assumptions. In many cases it doesn't mean that our assumptions weren't valid when we developed our model—just that things have changed since then. It's quite possible that assumptions made by a 13 year old, while valid at the time, no longer apply to the same person at age 55.

All mental models are based on assumptions. Assumptions are the glue that holds a conceptual model together. We make thousands of assumptions every day, often without even realizing it. The more aware we are of our assumptions, the less rigid our thinking.

I recommend that organizations acknowledge the power of language by using assumptive language. This process both volunteers and solicits assumptions during normal conversation. Using expressions like "Assuming that..." or "What are your assumptions regarding..." helps identify the underlying assumptions that color our thinking.

By the way, next time you set your alarm clock, realize that you are assuming it will in fact go off at the intended time.

> *It's always wise to raise questions about the most obvious and simple assumptions.*
>   ~ *C. West Churchman*

Time To Think

An obvious prerequisite to challenging one's thinking is finding the time to think. Regrettably, most leaders insist that they are too busy to engage in reflective thought. An environment that values action above reflection reinforces this perception. After all, leaders are expected to *carry the ball* and *deliver results*.

We live in a society where the oxymoron of *quick thinking* is cherished. As many a replaced CEO can testify, there is an unspoken "*and effective*" between "quick" and "thinking".

Thinking is essential to making good decisions; it is enhanced (and speeded up!) by conditions that support concentration. The best advice we can give to those leading change is to pause for thought a minimum of twice a day for at least 10 minutes. This is a prescription for slowing down to speed up—retreating from our frenetic workdays to concentrate on accelerating thought. It is far more productive to consume a few minutes a day in dedicated thinking than to waste hours embroiled in the latest crisis.

Multi-tasking has its place, but multi-tasking is about doing, not thinking. Conceptual thinking is best done when all of one's mental capacity can be focused on the problem at hand.

> *Just because we increase the speed of information doesn't mean we can increase the speed of decisions. Pondering, reflecting and ruminating are undervalued skills in our culture.*
> ~ *Dale Dauten*

Think At A System Level

It's easy to get caught up with the alligators rather than focusing on the swamp-draining mission. The ramifications of implementing change are difficult to predict. We have trouble seeing them because our 500-year heritage of mechanistic thought has conditioned us to study the parts in order to understand the machine.

Often, however, the behavior of the whole cannot be anticipated from studying the parts. These unforeseen system characteristics are called *emergent properties*. For example, even if we study the human eye and understand how it works, it is unlikely that we would predict the emergent property of three-dimensional vision. Three-dimensional vision is created not by the eye but by the relationship between two eyes and the brain. We can learn this only by studying the whole system.

During change, unanticipated consequences can arise that discourage us and threaten the stickiness of the change. If we challenge ourselves to think at a system level, we improve our ability to anticipate interactions and avoid being surprised by unexpected consequences.

Unexpected Consequences

I once took a course in systems thinking. The instructor challenged us to come up with an example of a system that accomplished its design intention but later produced unexpected consequences.

One fellow had just purchased a house in the country and spoke about finding a 50 lb. bag of animal feed in the garage. Inquiring of the former owners, he learned that they had bought the feed to put out in the winter so the deer wouldn't eat the shrubs.

That first winter he started putting the feed out and everything was fine until he realized that all the food was gone and the shrubs were beginning to disappear. He increased the amount of food and the plan worked again, yet after a brief delay the shrubs once more began to vanish. The solution apparently worked for a while and then stopped working.

I couldn't help but imagine the deer chattering in the woods. "Free dinner at the Jones's house!" He probably attracted every deer in the county.

This situation resembles many newly changed systems that seem to be working initially but then exhibit a delayed negative impact. I've seen many a manager on the fast track make the quick fixes and be promoted on the instant success, serendipitously missing the wake of delayed consequences. Did you ever wonder why a sales promotion at the end of the month to "hit the number" turns into below-forecast sales at the beginning of the next month?

Organizations are rarely improved by focusing on a single area or subset of areas. An organization is a collection of intimately connected relationships that combine to produce emergent properties and overall system performance.

Improvement in 21st century organizations requires integrated whole-organization solutions. It has become brutally clear that optimizing organizations locally often results in global sub-optimization. So beware of the purchasing department that wants to improve efficiency (their own) by restricting the ordering of supplies to the hour between 9:00 and 10:00 a.m.

Acknowledging the importance of systems encourages us to challenge our thinking regarding the impact of our solutions. This shift in thinking parallels scientific thought as it expands from Newtonian reductionist thinking to more generative systems thinking. Challenge yourself to think in wholes rather than in parts.

toɘ⌿ɘЯReflect

Challenge yourself to think reflectively also. During change, events occur that do not exactly meet our expectations. Try to reflect on the situation before judging prematurely. I often ask leaders to consider that the system always works perfectly. **If things didn't turn out the way we expected, we probably don't fully understand how the system really works.** By reflecting on what happened we have an opportunity to understand the interaction of the pieces of the system and their relationship to each other.

As a plant manager I once had to resolve an unfortunate incident that occurred on the second shift. A threat by a new employee had ultimately escalated to fisticuffs. It was easy to judge the actions of the participants harshly. But reflecting on how the system had perfectly delivered the undesirable result uncovered flaws in the hiring process, off-shift policies, and training. If those were not changed it was likely that a similar situation would occur again.

It is important to ask ourselves about our own relationship to whatever system we are reflecting upon. Our scientific training has created the illusion that we can be independent observers. In truth, it is virtually impossible to observe a system without affecting it. For example, consider whether the act of benchmarking a best practice affects the performance of those being benchmarked. How much does benchmarking improve the practice being studied? Will the best practice diminish when the benchmarking stops?

Managing by exception focuses our thinking and energy on events that have fallen short of expectations. There is, however, an opportunity for breakthrough thinking in reflecting on things that have gone unexpectedly well. Years ago I had a conversation with Ralph Stayer of Johnsonville Foods regarding the tasting of the sausage produced in their factory. After reflecting on his many roles he decided to let the people who made the sausage taste the sausage. Besides preventing unacceptable sausage from leaving the factory, they unexpectedly began to identify when the sausage tasted particularly good and how to reproduce that improved taste.

> *To reflect is to disturb one's thoughts.*
> *~ Jean Rostand*

Questions To Ponder

? Under what conditions does my thinking lose flexibility?

? Do I stop to think at least once a day? If not, what can I do to establish this discipline?

? Are there aspects of this change that people are viewing as either/or? If so, how can I encourage both/and thinking?

? What are my assumptions about this change?

? How is my thinking affecting my ability to accept the change? In what ways might my thinking be inhibiting the change?

? Would others describe me as open-minded?

? How am I affecting the current change?

? How will the change affect the performance of the whole system?

Putting The Principle Into Practice

 Some things *are* impossible... the way we see them now!

 Consider which aspects of the principles have to do with "Me" and which have to do with "We" (Hint: none are about "Us" and "Them").

 Ask questions that reframe the current context.

 Learn how to ask questions that cause others to think, such as, "What would have to happen for 'both/and' to be true?"

 Brainstorm less obvious consequences and benefits of proposed changes.

 Practice using assumptive language like:
My assumption is...
What are your assumptions?
What can we assume about this situation?
What might their assumptions be?
What might be incorrect about our assumptions?

 Remember that you cannot observe change without affecting the change.

 Allocate daily quiet time specifically for thinking.

 Learn more about systems thinking.

3 Involve And Be Involved

Tell me and I will forget. Show me and I will remember. Involve me and I will understand.
~ Confucius

THE surest road to commitment is to involve those affected by the change in its design and implementation. This involvement must not be window dressing but an authentic invitation to full participation. The participation encompasses the *how* of getting to the desired future state rather than any further discussion about whether the organization should change (although any genuine show-stoppers that emerge should be carefully considered).

Changes to job tasks typically involve a multitude of details. Those who do the work are best positioned to develop and tune these tasks because they are aware of both the goal and the day-to-day issues. When the people affected are involved, they are more likely to perceive the change as theirs, implement it in spite of obstacles, and ensure that it is sustained.

Not everyone is emotionally ready to be involved in the process. This is particularly true if trust levels in the organization are low. We must often take time to rebuild bridges before expecting people to become fully engaged and committed to change. Repeated acts of high integrity, *walking the talk*, will be required to build the levels of trust necessary to proceed.

You must, as Gandhi said, *be the change*. Pay attention to your actions and act consistently with the change. Try to anticipate and identify any misperceptions and defuse them with effective two-way communication. Top-down communication must be supplanted by communication more biased toward bottom-up. Two parts listening and one part talking is an excellent place to start. A good practice is to keep in mind Stephen Covey's habit of seeking first to understand and then be understood. Trust is earned by small daily acts over time, so don't wait to start.

Empathy Is Not A Dirty Word

Many people are hesitant to participate because they come from organizations (and families) that not only didn't solicit their input but may even have slain the messenger. Top leaders overcome this potential obstacle by mastering the art of empathy. I've seen many managers shy away from showing empathy. I believe their concern about empathy comes from a fear that they may appear weak or be perceived as expressing agreement or approval.

Empathy is trying to see the situation through the eyes of the other person. It doesn't mean you have to agree, only that you are attempting to understand how and why others feel the way they do.

> *Imagine that after a decade of working for the organization you have just been invited to the conference room for the first time. In ten years no one has ever asked for your opinion about anything. How might you feel when you walked into that room?*

Answering a question like this may help us suspend our judgment if the individual doesn't contribute much during the first few meetings. Suspension of judgment is an important leadership skill for helping others become fully involved. When you suspend judgment and listen to others openly, they will notice.

> *Don't judge a man until you have walked two moons in his moccasins.*
> ~ *Native American proverb*

Suspension of judgment takes practice. We frequently misjudge others because of attribution error. This phenomenon takes place so universally and frequently that psychologists call it *fundamental attribution error*. We are more likely to assume that other people's actions are related to their attitude and/or personality rather than to the environmental and social factors acting on them.

For example, we are more inclined to attribute a person's tardiness to "not caring" than to heavy traffic, car trouble, or failure to receive the revised meeting notice. When observing others, not knowing their situation, we myopically focus on the *kind* of person we think we're observing. Conversely, when evaluating our own actions we are likely to take into account all of the situational factors. If we reverse our thinking and first assume that people's behavior is substantially influenced by circumstances, we can enhance our ability to suspend judgment.

Encourage involvement by creating an environment in which people feel safe speaking out and believe that their input is understood and appreciated. **Allow anything to be questioned without repercussions**. Be aware that this is not always easy, particularly for those who built the current structure. Questions about the current system may feel like a personal affront comparable to being told that you have an ugly child. Prepare for this gut-level reaction and learn not to take questions personally.

Our bodies transmit our true emotions quite effectively. Studies have shown that over 50% of the meaning of our communications is expressed by our bodies. Our body language, tone of voice, language and intended meaning are intimately connected. I tested this with inside sales people and found that they could improve their phone sales if they sat up in their chairs as though they were face to face with the client. It's almost impossible to communicate enthusiasm with a slumped body. The impact of body language is significant and cannot be ignored. The good news is that as we modify our thinking, our body language automatically follows.

Involvement is essential to making change stick. However, involvement is not simply asking for input but creating an environment where people are not afraid to participate and commit fully. During change the probability of fear increases: rules become less clear, high-risk experiments are undertaken, and people are challenged to learn new things. People may feel particularly vulnerable during this period, which makes the job of creating a safe environment during change more difficult but even more important.

The No-Ring Circus

Joe was a line supervisor in a factory that made vacuum tubes. His department had several assembly lines, each containing a crew of five and a large machine that created vacuum in the tubes and then melted and sealed the glass. Morale was low and the machines were old and dirty; broken glass was everywhere. Joe wanted to clean things up but had trouble getting cooperation from the crews in completing even the simplest of cleaning plans.

One day Joe had a revelation. He went to the crews on each line and offered to let them name their machines and paint them any color they wanted. He also said they could decide on a plan to keep them neat and clean. Within days the machines had been cleaned and painted by the operators, name signs made, cleaning tools bought and cleaning plans put in motion. Every machine was immaculate with not a single shard of glass to be found anywhere. Morale and productivity increased; the improvements were sustained for several months.

The president of the company heard about the increased productivity and decided to walk through the department and see what was going on. When he saw the pink, green, and purple machines he admonished Joe, telling him that this was a place of business and not a circus. He ordered Joe to have the machines repainted battleship gray over the weekend before any customers showed up.

That Monday the machines were neat, clean and gray. Within two weeks, however, productivity had declined, the machines were dirty and full of glass, and morale had plummeted to a record low.

Questions To Ponder

? How am I involved with this change?

? How should my behaviors change to model excellence in the new system?

? Am I involving others as equal partners in the change?

? How much am I listening as compared to talking?

? What might others be feeling right now?

? Think of a time in your life when you were excluded from being involved. What did it feel like to be excluded? How does it feel to be included?

? Am I truly allowing others to participate openly? How can I confirm this?

Putting The Principle Into Practice

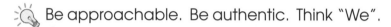 Once direction has been set, clearly communicate the goal and involve those who will be affected in determining the *how*.

 Be approachable. Be authentic. Think "We".

Talk personally to individuals as well as groups.

Be open to input from everyone. Ask opinions and solicit ideas. Listen intently.

Build trust by saying what you will do and doing what you say. Hold yourself accountable for being on time. Don't expect people to understand if you don't deliver.

Identify yourself with the change.

Do your homework. If people aren't participating, figure out why.

Reduce barriers to involvement. This can include things such as furniture placement and shape, seating position, technical language, acronyms, etc. Try wherever possible to level the playing field. Go visit the area and the people affected by the change.

4 Align Your Culture

Insanity: doing the same thing over and over again and expecting different results.

~ *Albert Einstein*

CULTURE is the gravitational field of an organization. For most people, organizational culture lurks in the background and is rarely noticed or talked about. Its effects, however, are profound. Culture reflects organizational history and the core values of leadership. It acts as a filter for desirable attitudes and behaviors. It is impossible to change any part of the organization without passing cultural muster. Leadership groups within the organization establish the unique aspects of the local culture. **Systemic changes usually require a change in local culture to allow new behaviors and attitudes to take hold.**

It has been my experience that culture cannot be changed unless leadership also changes its attitudes and behaviors. This fact is often overlooked. Leadership decisions regarding who must change often communicate an "*I'm OK, you're not OK*" attitude to the rest of the organization. This is an unhealthy parent-child transactional model. Amazingly, I've actually had supervisors ask me why the people reporting to them act so much like children—an illustration of the Pygmalion effect at its best.

A Lock On Trust

I had an appointment with the president of a high-profile manufacturer servicing the printing industry. After entering the lobby and signing in, I began to notice something unusual.

The receptionist's desk drawers, cabinets, and file drawers all had very obvious locks that she was constantly locking and unlocking as I stood there waiting. Looking around the room, I noticed more and more locks and a tiny camera looking back at me. I was thankful when the president's assistant finally emerged through a locked door to escort me to his office.

Once I was safely inside, the president asked if I'd like a cup of coffee. When I nodded, he pushed a button under his desk to summon a woman named Elvira. I couldn't help but notice a key ring the size of a Wild West jailer's attached to her side with a mountaineer's carabiner. The president and I walked with her to the cafeteria where she unlocked a cabinet to get me a cup and another to get the supplies to make the coffee. While the coffee was brewing the president suggested that we take a quick tour of the plant.

In the shop, the president's tour was a heads-down, task-focused whirlwind. His lack of personal engagement with the workers was blatantly obvious and apparently legendary. He did not speak to anyone except me. As I was stopping to say hello to the people in each area he was pressing along to the next workstation with a disapproving scowl. I couldn't help but notice the cameras mounted on the walls of the shop, just like the one I saw in the lobby.

Back in his office we discussed the type of assistance he wanted as I sipped the coffee that Elvira had delivered. He was extremely critical of the people working in his organization and bemoaned the caliber of the help. "Why can't I find trustworthy people?"

As I left, I peeked into the cafeteria. Elvira had just finished washing my coffee cup and was locking it back up in one of the 20 locked cabinets lining the cafeteria walls.

Culture Governs Behavior

If organizational culture is incompatible with a change, the change will not stick. It can be difficult to appreciate the effect of culture on organizational behavior but we underestimate it at our peril; **culture affects every member of the organization.**

Complexity theory with its concept of self-organizing systems provides a model for understanding how culture governs the behavior of organizations. Contained within the theory is a phenomenon called the *strange attractor*. A strange attractor is the focus of a pattern of seemingly chaotic behavior. The attractor itself has no tangible characteristics and can only be inferred by the pattern created around it.

Looking at the collection of behaviors exhibited in an organization reveals patterns that imply a set of governing forces within the culture. Those governing forces affect how we think about our organization (our mind-set) and ultimately how we behave.

How often have you returned from a seminar full of enthusiasm, only to lose it within minutes of returning to the office? It happens so frequently and universally that I call it the *seminar effect*. When we are overwhelmed by the status quo, it's no wonder our hunger for improvement is so quickly dampened.

Organizations exhibit an inertia that causes them to stay the same despite efforts to move them forward. It's as if some invisible force pulls us back from the new and exciting ideas that stimulated our imaginations only hours before.

The same forces that cause the seminar effect play a role in preventing change from sticking. You can hear it in the language of resignation as our teammates proclaim, "That's the way things are around here; nothing ever changes." The language is helpless and can easily become a self-fulfilling prophecy. This attitude has often been reinforced by a long parade of "flavor-of-the-month" programs that quickly went supernova before the workers' eyes. If the strange attractors of an organizational culture are preventing needed change, then something must be done to modify the system.

The Boundary Dilemma

The tiny signals being sent and received within every organization are invisible and ubiquitous. We are so immersed in our environment that it's almost impossible to recognize all of the forces that can subvert change. It is usually the combined effect of many subtle attractors that keeps individuals and groups within manageable boundaries (and keeps unwanted change out).

These boundaries represent the current organizational paradigm or culture; people must remain within the boundaries to achieve success. For the most part this is helpful since it answers our questions about "what we have to do to be successful around here."

But boundaries cause difficulties when the organization must move to a place on the far side of the moat. Then, like an inflating balloon, the boundary resists with increasing force as we attempt to expand the change within the organization. The strange attractors within the organization pull people away from the change. The system, while working perfectly as designed, is yielding an undesirable result and therefore must be altered.

The transparent but effective boundaries that exist in every organization are created by concepts, policies, practices, values and mores of leadership, and even by legends created about the founders. It is critical to understand the influence of these signals on the organization at large. To achieve a change that sticks, we must expand the boundaries to encompass the desired change. For example, to create an organization of lifelong learners, recognize and reward individuals for learning and not solely for seniority.

To become more aware of the subtle forces at work, we must investigate the forces that are both driving and resisting the change. A force field diagram, originally developed by Kurt Lewin, is a good tool for graphically recording this analysis. If nothing is changing, the forces will be in equilibrium. In order to advance toward the goal the driving forces must be increased and/or the restraining forces must be diminished.

Driving Forces		Restraining Forces
Involvement	→←	Fear
Compelling Reason	→←	Mistrust
Recognition	→←	Poor Communication
Clear Measurements	→←	Cultural Inertia
Leadership Support	→←	Leadership Inconsistencies
Tolerance for Errors	→←	Criticism
Teamwork	→←	Personal Agendas
Personal Accountability	→←	Victimizers

Figure 4.1. Force Field Diagram

Even when the signals are realigned, the inertia of the old system continues to resist change; time and incentives are required to move the organization in the desired direction. When the rules change, it takes effort to untrain and retrain. The more ingrained the rule, the more difficult it is to change.

I must confess that in the early 1980s as a plant manager for 3M, I thought my supervisor had lost his mind when he suggested the concept of manufacturing a batch size of one. His suggestion made absolutely no sense to me; I just couldn't see it, so I resisted it. Paradoxically, today a sizable percentage of my consulting practice involves helping clients achieve that elusive batch size of one.

Leadership Creates Culture

Over time, leadership creates formal and informal rules that become the boundaries for acceptable behavior in the organization. The daily actions of leaders clarify, nullify, or augment these rules by providing subtle signals concerning what is or is not really appreciated.

The well-known expression "walk the talk" is clear recognition of this power of behavioral influence, while "Do as I say, not as I do" provides a humorous acknowledgment of how difficult it is to modify our behavior consistent with change. Here lies the truth of why change often does not stick.

Because culture is so pervasive and its effects so strong, an honest examination of organizational culture is an essential prerequisite to any change initiative. Cultural dissonance can sabotage the best-planned change before it ever gets off the ground. Any notable disparity between the existing culture and the forces needed to motivate the change should be a warning flag to change leaders. If you want your change to stick, you may first need to focus significant effort on modifying the culture to support the change.

Cultural transformation is a major undertaking because it affects the foundational thinking, values, and principles of the organization and those who lead it. Culture cannot be transformed without motivation, revelation and an associated internal change within the leaders involved. For most people, this is a difficult personal transition.

Do Fish Know They Live In Water?

I received a call from a client complaining that his company had tried to implement teams but it just wasn't working. Would I stop by and take a look at what happened?

During my meeting, I asked Bill to walk me through the implementation process. He pulled a company-wide memo out of a file and handed it to me. The first few paragraphs discussed the issues in the marketplace, how competition was getting tougher and collaboration was the only approach to survival.

I was favorably impressed until I reached the end of the memo where it stated in no uncertain terms, "Effective Monday, everyone must be a team player."

Next, Bill offered a memo that he had sent to all managers. It also had a zinger at its end: "Anyone who is not a team player should be coached, demoted, or replaced."

With my interest piqued, I continued the investigation by asking what happened next. Bill explained how he had read that an open office layout would help stimulate collaboration. I acknowledged that I also had heard this and was eager to hear his results.

He explained that this was a top priority so he picked his best facilities ace for the project. In a matter of days they had conceived a plan to level every office in the building.

I couldn't help but envision the herd of dazed refugee engineers bumping into each other, perplexed by what had happened to their workplace over the weekend. When I asked why he hadn't included the people affected in the office design, he said that this was a business crisis and there just wasn't time for such niceties.

By now I was a little afraid to hear his views on recognition, but I couldn't resist asking. He said, "I read that leaders should catch someone doing something right and reward them."

"Excellent plan! Did you find a team with extraordinary performance?" He replied, "Yes, I did. John really made his team perform, so in appreciation I immediately promoted him to a supervisory position."

There was no doubt in my mind that Bill had good intentions, properly diagnosed the problem and selected an appropriate solution. Unfortunately, the implementation missed the target by a mile.

Trying to put a new concept into place using the old rules, rewards, and unsupportive culture will rarely work.

For new growth to take root the soil must be tested, tilled, and correctly fertilized prior to planting new seeds. Once rooted, to grow and bear fruit they must receive periodic doses of sun and water appropriate for their kind.

Aligning organizational culture with the change is arguably the most critical element in the formula for stickiness. Align your rainbow's end with the new desired state and your organization will be irresistibly attracted there to stay.

> *On a group of theories one can found a school;*
> *but on a group of values one can found a culture.*
> *~ Ignazio Silone*

Questions To Ponder

? How do my actions and attitudes influence the culture of this organization?

? What pressures am I feeling that work against the change?

? Am I avoiding certain aspects of the change? If so, what aspects and why?

? In what ways will our culture have to change? What aspects of the current culture will be most difficult for people to let go of?

? What do I feel is unfair about the change? Which of my values causes me to have this feeling?

? What do I feel is good about the change?

Putting The Principle Into Practice

 If you cannot "walk the talk", look for the cultural obstacles preventing the walk.

 Determine what mind-set is necessary to deliver the new desired performance, then identify the components of your culture that encourage or discourage that mind-set.

 Consider what would motivate people to exhibit the mind-set needed to deliver the new performance. Would using that motivator as a reinforcement be consistent or inconsistent with the existing organizational culture? Would anyone in leadership think the reinforcement inappropriate?

 If you uncover a conflict between a core value and the desired mind-set, think about whether the discord is related to the value itself or the way the value is interpreted. Changing the interpretation is far easier than changing the value.

 If you see behaviors that support the old system rather than the new, ask "What is the incentive for this person to continue this behavior?"

The ghosts of former leaders linger. Change may be inhibited by historic cultural signals that no longer make sense in the current context. Be a ghost buster by detecting and correcting misperceptions in the organization.

When you decide to change a cultural signal, determine what leadership behaviors would most effectively communicate that change and hold each other accountable. How does a habit of being late to meetings fit in an organization that is trying to encourage responsiveness and on-time delivery?

5 Honor Emotions

It is not so much that we are afraid of change or so in love with the old ways, but it's that place in between that we fear…. It's like being caught between trapezes. It's Linus when his blanket is in the dryer. There's nothing to hold on to.

~ Marilyn Ferguson

It's important to recognize that along with the physical and intellectual aspects of change we also must go through the emotional experience of transition. Transition is the psychological process of coming to grips with new circumstances. Change will not stick if transition does not occur.

Like the process of mourning, negotiating transition requires us to let go and leave some very comfortable things behind. It may be the comfort of knowing our old job really well or perhaps just where we park or when we go to lunch.

Difficulties occur because we can rarely let go of our security blanket and immediately replace it with a new one that feels just as good. We leave the comfortable for the unknown of transition, the place between trapezes.

In transition the old rules no longer apply and the new rules are still in flux. We try to deny that anything is happening until the change becomes inescapable. Our feelings continue to evolve through frustration, resistance, and even anger. Some people choose to struggle—to remain comfortably uncomfortable—rather than face the apprehensions and discomforts associated with transition.

Although organizational change is a group activity, transition remains a solitary journey. The choices of transition are personal; we cannot make them for others. We must give up the illusion that we can change other people; only they can choose whether or not to accept a change. We can influence others' choices by not dismissing or belittling the emotional challenges they are experiencing.

Those who initiate and champion a change are not immune to the pangs of transition. No matter how fast we are moving, the emotions of transition ultimately catch up. Being initiators does not exempt us from having to let go of something that is familiar and most likely comfortable. Vested in the new idea, we are enthusiastic and our intellects tend to lull us into believing we're just fine. A day will come, however, when the inventory of what we have lost will be counted.

> *All changes, even the most longed for, have their melancholy; for what we leave behind us is a part of ourselves; we must die to one life before we can enter another.* ~ *Anatole France*

The Day of Reckoning

It was a beautiful spring morning in 1993 and I was on my way to work. We had just implemented a redesign of the entire operations organization. I had conceived the plan in an attempt to reverse a negative performance trend and improve on-time deliveries.

For more than a year my colleagues and I had studied World Class manufacturing organizations; we felt we had designed a unique and effective way to run the business. The work was intellectually stimulating and everything seemed to be going great.

I opened the door and walked the dark hallway to my office. Across the aisle were the skeletal remains of my department—a massive field of empty desks illuminated by the sun peeking through the window blinds. No lights, no noise, no people, no life. Forty-nine of the 50 people reporting to me had been reassigned to self-directed teams. As the key turned in the lock on my office door I felt in my gut a new and painful feeling of loss. What had I done?

Resilience Is Crucial

Big changes in our lives often just happen and we are left to endure the tempest that follows. Some people weather the storm of change better than others. We all know people who have bounced back from unfathomable losses and changes like trees that bend without snapping in a hurricane. Somehow these people have developed a marvelous survival skill called resilience.

Daryl Conner, in his seminal work *Managing at the Speed of Change*[2], identified a number of common characteristics of resilient people. In particular, five characteristics seem to stand out: resilient people are focused, positive, flexible, organized, and proactive.

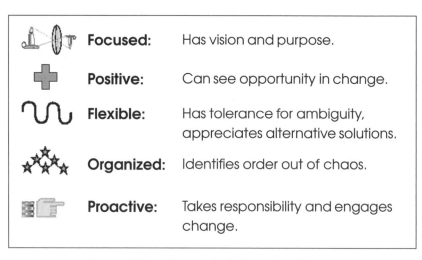

Figure 5.1. Characteristics of Resilience

I believe that resilience can be developed to reduce the trauma of transition. From personal experience I do not believe that the impact of change can be eliminated, but the depth of the chasm between old and new can be effectively reduced. Certainly we can do a better job of supporting each other through the change process. Many organizations, oblivious to the implications of unsupported change, unwittingly strap people into the corporate equivalent of Disney's Space Mountain roller coaster in the dark.

Loss And Opportunity

William Bridges, in his book *Transitions: Making Sense of Life's Changes* [3], introduced a change model that contains three phases described as endings, neutral zone, and new beginnings.

Interestingly, during the ending and neutral phases many of the emotions parallel those experienced in the five-stage mourning process described by Elisabeth Kubler-Ross in her book *On Death and Dying* [4]. In a sense, systemic change can be an end to organizational life as we know it.

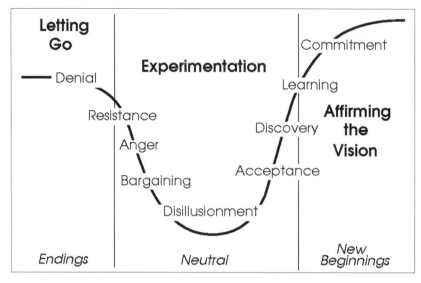

Figure 5.2. Emotions During Transition

While the ambiguity of the neutral zone may be unsettling, it is a time when constraints are diminished and **creativity can flourish**. Creativity is often hindered by the existing systemic order. The chaos of the neutral zone weakens the biases of the status quo and provides an excellent opportunity to encourage innovation. Our top priority should be getting everyone safely through the transition, but we shouldn't ignore these optimum conditions for stimulating creativity.

There are opportunities to ease the journey in each phase. Behavioral style differences provide individual talents and potential weaknesses at different points on the change curve. Knowledge of behavioral styles can help in determining who should lead the charge at each stage of the process.

There are a number of four-factor behavioral models in the marketplace that are variations on a similar theme. Most of the modern work on this subject is traceable to the 1928 book *Emotions of Normal People* [5] by William Moulton Marston. According to Marston, "All people exhibit all four behavioral factors in varying degrees of intensity."

The factors he chose (from which **DISC** theory takes its name) were **Dominance, Inducement, Submission,** and **Compliance**. Evolution of the theory has replaced the word *Inducement* with **Influence** and *Submission* with **Steadiness**.

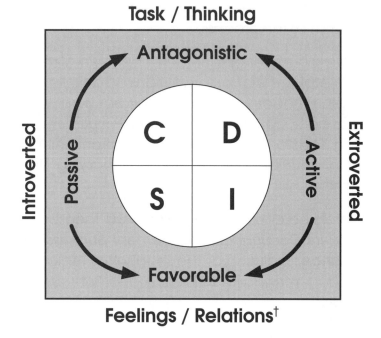

Figure 5.3. DISC Behavioral Factors

- **Dominance** becomes active in an antagonistic environment

- **Influence** becomes active in a favorable environment

- **Steadiness** becomes passive in a favorable environment

- **Compliance** becomes passive in an antagonistic environment [†]

[†]adapted from material © 1993, 2004, Target Training International, Ltd. [6]

Generally speaking, people with introverted behavioral styles are more apt to be disturbed by change and resist it than those who are extroverted. Those most severely affected are frequently the most steady, solid, and loyal organizational citizens. They rarely show their true feelings publicly for fear of disrupting relationships. Poker-faced, they may become paralyzed until the need for the change is understood and internalized.

Those who are more rule-bound and data-driven are concerned about the effects of change and often will resist more openly. The reaction of both styles makes sense since during transition existing rules soften, new rules are not yet written, and things seem to be happening way too fast.

Task-focused extroverts are frequently initiators and drivers of change. People-oriented extroverts are often flexible and can sometimes even be oblivious to change.

To avoid a lengthy discussion of behavior styles, just imagine that you have a group of four people facing an organizational change: *D*on Tell, *I*ris Sell, *S*am Steady, and *C*indy Careful. During the change Tell, Sell, Steady and Careful each experience and are affected by the phases of change quite differently.

Tell and Sell are outspoken and early advocates of the change. Tell is anxious to get going and doesn't want to be bothered with the details. Sell has lots of enthusiasm and tries to win over Steady and Careful.

Careful is in a bit of a dither since she sees Sell as a lot of hype and not much substance. Careful says she has been burned before by Sell, who tends to over-delegate and under-instruct. Sell, however, has apparently helped Steady with her explanation of the problem and the reasons why change is needed to resolve the problem.

Steady and Careful are nonetheless very concerned. Careful is convinced that Sell and Tell haven't taken everything into account. Steady thinks that things are moving too fast but doesn't want to burden anyone with his problem so he tries not to show his emotions. Sell says she read a book about change and the first phase of the change is when we have to let go of the comfortable. Tell appears nervous and on edge; sometimes he is very quick to anger.

Some of Steady's departmental peers seem to be in denial, still saying that the change isn't going to happen. Steady has gotten past that stage but is experiencing a deep sense of loss as he enters transition. He's struggling and talking with his wife about it at night. Careful is getting frustrated and angry with Tell and Sell since all they seem to do is talk in generalities without providing a clear plan for forward motion.

Tell and Sell think that Steady and Careful are being resistant and don't want to change. Tell is now pushing way too hard and has some people scared out of their wits. Careful has discovered that Steady is very empathetic and a great listener. Steady is happy to support others who are upset and confused. While he isn't clear himself, he feels a sense of satisfaction and belonging when he's involved one-on-one.

Careful has become a bit sarcastic and partially paralyzed since all the rules about how to do things have disappeared. Sell has decided to hold weekly pizza lunches that people can come to just to share time and enjoy the camaraderie. The plan seems to help everyone feel a little better but does little for the change's forward motion.

Just when things are looking quite bleak, Tell mysteriously comes to the rescue. Tell's clear directions and strong leadership seem to bring order to the mess. Careful is asked to work out some new procedures and processes and puts considerable effort into it. Sell has dusted off the vision and people are actually starting to think they're going to get there. Steady gets a surprise MVP award at Sell's pizza luncheon for being such a solid team player and doing pretty much whatever needs to be done to move the change forward.

The Emotional Dynamics Of Change

Future-focused leaders often think that the fix for the sliding morale of transition is just to get everyone fired up about the exciting new future ahead of them. Failure to consider the emotional impact of change is a major factor in the derailment of the change process.

How interested would you be in talking about tonight's dinner menu while you're headed down that roller coaster in the dark? It's difficult to think when you're trying not to scream. So why is it socially acceptable to express one's emotional state at the amusement park and not on the even scarier ride at work? In varying degrees, **everyone has emotional reactions to change.** Individuals can be supported through the change process by acknowledging these emotions and permitting their open expression.

It's also important to remind people that in most changes we are not leaving everything behind. Some of the things we collect in our lives become old and worn out while others become valuable antiques. Dump the junk and relish the antiques.

Acknowledge transition by ritualizing the passage if possible. In *Why God Won't Go Away* [7], neurobiologist Andrew Newberg, M.D. concludes that our brains are hard-wired for rituals. Anthropologists have long acknowledged the important survival function of rituals. Rituals help us feel special, connected, and identify us as members of the clan.

> *Ceremony and ritual spring from our*
> *heart of hearts: those who govern us know*
> *it well, for they would sooner deny us bread*
> *than dare alter the observance of tradition.*
> ~ F. Gonzalez-Crussi

Merge Right

Halfway through a management seminar I was teaching, the General Manager was informed that the company had been acquired. Serendipitously, my seminar contained a section on change and transition. I was invited to help design a plan to support people through the change.

The company had been in business for decades and many people had spent all or a good part of their careers there; they identified themselves with the organization. We discussed ritualizing the company's name change to make it more a passing of the torch than a funeral.

We were a little too late. Over the weekend, the acquiring company replaced the name on the front of the building with their own.

Later in the transition process we held meetings to allow people to express their feelings. In every meeting someone mentioned how empty, disconnected, and "sold out" they felt when the new sign surprised them as they drove into the parking lot. For many, that surprise signified the death of what they belonged to and the beginning of a period of mourning. Ritualizing the name change could have reduced the pain.

dx/dt

It's also important to recognize that we don't all go through transition at the same pace or the same time. An organization is like a long train traveling down one hill and up the next; the locomotive can be at the crest of the second hill while the caboose is still descending the first one. Management usually initiates organizational change and transitions through it first. I encourage leaders to realize that just because they feel fine and have successfully negotiated the journey doesn't mean that others in the organization have, or that there is anything "wrong" with those who have not yet arrived.

Change and transition affect each of us differently based on our perception of its impact on us. Our response is within our control, although it may not always feel that way. We can see change as a problem or an opportunity. By the way, most of those resilient people are home making lemonade with all those lemons they've been dealt. We choose whether to adopt the posture of a victim, opportunist, or team player.

> *We see the world not as it is, but as we are.*
> ~ *the Talmud*

Our ability to endure transition has much to do with the way we think. The flexible tree usually survives the storm while the rigid one may not. During large systemic change we undoubtedly will be faced with having to revise some aspects of our thinking. If you think giving things up is tough, buckle your seat belt; adopting new concepts is even more difficult. Our mental models have been developed and refined over years of experience. Each refinement reinforces the concept and stiffens the bulwarks against attack (notice the metaphors!). Change will never stick in a worldview that precludes the change.

The essence of sticky change involves creating an environment in which individuals can work through the process of understanding the change rather than just having to accept it. The changes that organizations undertake frequently require radical shifts in thinking. Trusted paradigms come under attack. Often the new principles are the antithesis of those that were conventional wisdom for most of the 20th century. Increasingly, people engaging change will experience substantial cognitive dissonance.

People resist learning things that contradict what they think they already know, especially if they have been strongly vested in that knowledge. The level of discomfort is directly related to the perceived discrepancy between what is known and what must now be assimilated. Addressing perceptual accuracy and establishing points of similarity between the old and the new before discussing differences can avert unnecessary grief. Even the best-case scenarios, however, still require substantial mental realignment.

Questions To Ponder

? How do I feel about the change?

? What do I need to let go of as a result of this change?

? Where do I think I am on the change curve right now? Where do I think others in the organization are?

? How do I feel about the people who appear to be resisting the change?

? What actions could I take to ease the transition for myself? For others?

? What rituals are part of the current organizational culture? Which ones can continue after the change? What new rituals can be instituted to replace old ones?

? What can I do to help develop the characteristics of resilience in myself and others?

Putting The Principle Into Practice

It's likely that the new desired attitudes and behaviors already exist in your organization. Look for examples and use them to ease fears and to develop models for the future.

Become a student of behavioral styles and the change process by observing your own behavior and others' during the change. Don't expect everyone to experience the transition the same way you do, or to be at the same place on the curve.

While behaviors are classifiable by direct observation, formal assessment provides a more accurate measurement of the intensity of each behavioral factor and gives insight into how the factors interact. Knowing the behavioral styles of individuals can help during transition and also during team selection. It makes sense to balance teams with a variety of behavioral styles.

Implement rituals within the organization. Small rituals such as a regular monthly meeting to talk about how things are going or to acknowledge exemplary performance help people feel like part of the community. A useful ritual can be as simple as walking through the office every Friday just to say hello.

Storytelling can be highly effective as a change catalyst in even the most change-resistant organizations. Telling an appropriate story can stimulate people to think about the implications of change. Stories can help us understand what it might be like to do things differently.

When you ask how others are doing, use language that solicits emotional feedback. Rather than asking what people *think* about the change, try asking how they *feel* about it. This modification in wording is subtle yet significant. Don't ask either question unless you are prepared to listen to the response with empathy.

There are many combinations and permutations of the four DISC behavioral factors. I have found no single pattern that is strong during all the phases of transition. Each of us possesses a behavioral pattern that can help during some stages of transition and cause potential derailment during other stages.

The most effective changes occur when everyone in the organization works together to capitalize on these differences by optimizing their personal strengths and minimizing their liabilities during change. For example, if you need accurate data collected, give the job to someone who is behaviorally suited for the task.

Core Style:	**Dominance**
Attitude Toward Change:	Likes change
Contributions During Change:	Limitations During Change:
• **Drive** • Risk-taking • Results-oriented • Self-starter • Tenacious • Forward-looking	• **Not a good listener** • Impatient with others • Confrontational • Too directive • Task-focused

Core Style:	**Influence**
Attitude Toward Change:	What change???
Contributions During Change:	Limitations During Change:
• **Enthusiasm** • Creative solutions • Humor • Team player • Articulate • Peacemaker	• **Talks more than listens** • May oversell • Not detail-oriented • Inadequate delegation • Poor time management

Core Style:	**Steadiness**
Attitude Toward Change:	Dislikes change

Contributions During Change:	Limitations During Change:
• **Empathetic** • Team player • Loyal & dependable • Great listener • Peacemaker • Logical	• **Waits for orders** • Internalizes feelings • May not take risks • Multi-tasking difficult • May passively resist change

Core Style:	**Compliance**
Attitude Toward Change:	Concerned about the effects

Contributions During Change:	Limitations During Change:
• **Detail-oriented** • Thorough & accurate • High standards • Fact-finder • Objective thinker • Asks good questions	• **Analysis paralysis** • Overly critical • May get defensive • Internalizes feelings • Task-focused

Confront Fear

Fear is a darkroom where negatives develop.

~ Usman Asif

FEAR is the greatest obstacle to change. Unlike other animals, humans have the capacity to anticipate danger. This can cause a stress response even when little threat exists. Animals become fearful only when danger is physically present; in humans the danger arousal system can be invoked based on the perception of potential danger. Organizational change plunges people into the unknown, which for many is synonymous with potential danger and fear.

Fear mushrooms in the dark corners of our minds. In silence, we fast-forward from the present and postulate "what-if" scenarios that arouse our fear response. Most of us have been brought up not to discuss our fears and perhaps not even to admit having them. We tend to hide our fears, which prevents us from discovering whether they are unfounded or exaggerated. Underlying fears can negatively affect our performance and supersede reality as the principal cause of failure.

The best way to combat our fears is to shine light on them. Ironically, this is exactly the thing we are most afraid to do.

Fear quickly becomes contagious and sometimes escalates into mass hysteria. Memorial Day in 1883 ended with 12 people trampled to death at the opening of the Brooklyn bridge when someone's fear of its falling was vocalized.

We must be keenly aware that fear is based on individual perception, which typically involves some fact and some fiction. Accurate information carefully communicated is the best countermeasure against fears created or exaggerated by misinformation, misperception, and ignorance.

At work, people often react to fear by adopting defensive strategies such as hiding, blaming, avoiding, stalling, bargaining, or even disappearing (absenteeism). It may seem that the blowing winds of amnesia have caused an epidemic of short-term memory loss and a return to the good old comfortable ways. People's heads may even move up and down in agreement while their feet remain firmly cemented to the ground.

Leadership is not immune. Fear of failure can sabotage the change process. A leader's attitude during change is crucially important to the mission: few people will follow a tentative leader into the unknown. The most lethal strains of contagious fear are the ones contracted and passed on by leadership.

The Only Thing We Have To Fear...

People fear many things during organizational change. Archetypal models of fear lurk in the baggage we bring to our jobs with us; corporate culture can reinforce old fear models and create new ones. I once heard a top executive say, "I don't want to know what happened, tell me who to blame." The idea of conducting a witch-hunt to find someone to blame didn't become a corporate stereotype by accident.

Fear of making a mistake is one of the major fears encountered during change because the probability of making mistakes is so dramatically increased. Those operating in a "Who did it?" culture should restructure their first question following a mistake from "Who?" to "What happened?" and ultimately end with a question about what was learned from the experience. It may, however, take a large bottle of antacids and a few days locked in the office to get the body language under control.

> *Slowness to change usually means fear of the new.*
> *~ Philip Crosby*

Many fears involve our concerns about how we appear to others. Since most changes require us to learn new things, fear of looking foolish or incompetent and fear of not being able to learn make frequent appearances during transition.

What If....

I remember being quite excited about the arrival of our plant's first personal computer. I could hardly wait to tell my administrative assistant that she could give up her old typewriter for a shiny new computer. But when I delivered the news she was immediately resistant and abruptly informed me that she was not going to switch; she said she saw no benefit to it.

After a few days of tension and a few rounds of discussion it became clear that she was afraid she couldn't master the new device and that she would look incompetent. In desperation I finally offered to let her take the computer home for a few weeks to play with it, assuring her that she could do nothing from the keyboard to break it.

Within one week the computer had returned and the typewriter was unceremoniously retired. Three years later this former technophobe left the company to start her own business teaching others to master the personal computer.

Even good intentions can inadvertently create fear. My first client, after generating a vision and mission statement with input from about 30% of the organization, felt that they had erred by not including everyone in the process.

To remedy the oversight they decided to shut down the company for an off-site meeting. The purpose of the event was to involve everyone in the company in discussion of the first draft. In 40 years of business the company had never been shut down on a workday before. The organizers felt this would send a strong message about the importance of the activity and management's commitment.

Despite efforts to communicate the event's purpose, on the day of the meeting several toolmakers and machinists were seen carrying their toolboxes to their cars, convinced that the company was going to inform everyone of its closing. In this case, it was the unusual pattern that created fear. Do you think it's uncommon for unusual patterns to occur during major systemic change?

History Can Hurt You

Fear is a conditioned response. Through repeated uncomfortable experiences most of us have subconsciously created a link between change and impending danger. Over time, that connection becomes hard-wired into our early warning system. Our fear stems in part from having to let go of some aspect of our current predictable conditions. It may be the loss of hard-earned expertise and its associated status or an erosion of our confidence when faced with new things to learn. Either way, we experience discomfort and a feeling of helplessness, especially when we perceive a loss of control.

A history of bad experiences also builds an expectation of failure and fear of yet another change. After a chain of failures, the more attractive the change is the more reluctant people will be to commit to it.

> *Scalded cats fear even cold water.*
> ~ *Thomas Fuller*

This reaction was clearly illustrated to me as a plant manager. The corporation had generously instituted a new eyeglass benefit for all employees. I was quite excited about it and conducted a very upbeat plant-wide meeting to describe it to the employees.

Following the meeting, several of our more outspoken employees requested a private meeting in my office. They were angry and said I had abused them in the meeting. Totally dumbfounded, I asked how. They replied that they knew another shoe would soon drop and they would ultimately lose more than they had gained in the exchange. They were particularly angry with me for being so optimistic and persuasive.

I was shocked that I could have done something good and lost their trust in the process. Only later did I realize that most of my workers were second- and third-generation factory workers from a large northeastern industrial city. They were brought up to believe that they should beware of companies trying to take advantage of them. They had been taught to be suspicious of anything that appeared too good. They had scalded grandparents.

> *That which is feared lessens by association.*
>   ~ *Ovid*

As children we were terrified the most by the imagined monsters of the night lurking in the dark unseen corners of the room. As adults we may prefer to stay in an uncomfortable but predictable environment rather than take a step into the unknown toward anticipated improvement. One method for decoupling the fear response from change requires repeated changes that occur without negative consequences. An even more effective method couples significant change with positive rewards.

The human brain reacts physiologically to fear by invoking the "fight or flight" arousal system. Before attempting to appeal to the intellect to exorcise the underlying fear, it's prudent to wait for heightened emotions to subside. People who are afraid are emotionally on edge and often have difficulty thinking straight. Gaining agreement at this point may be only briefly satisfying; individuals are likely to feel manipulated when they return to clear thinking. Make every effort to deal with fear when people are calm and can approach the presenting issue in a rational way.

Everyone has fears, particularly during transition. It is neither abnormal nor a sign of weakness: it is simply human. To reduce its impact we must determine the nature of our fear and assess the validity and magnitude of the threat. It is important to create an environment that allows people to feel safe enough to discuss their fears. Treating others with respect and compassion while sharing some of our own concerns is a good step toward encouraging others to reveal their fears. Confronting our fears forces them out of the darkness and defuses much of their power over us.

Become aware of the power of fear to affect behavior. Fear is the substance that can dissolve even the stickiest changes. **When change doesn't stick, rule out fear** as a possible cause before trying to treat the symptom.

Questions To Ponder

? In what ways might I be contributing to the fears of others?

? How do I react when other people make mistakes? What is my first question?

? Whose behavior has visibly changed?

? Has anyone become abnormally quiet?

? What roles in the organization are changing the most? What can I do to help the people in those positions?

? Do I have fears about this change? What are they? With whom can I discuss them?

? How is morale in my work area? What can I do to improve it?

? Who is required to learn new skills? What are we doing to facilitate that effort?

? How can I create an environment in which people feel safe discussing their fears?

Putting The Principle Into Practice

Begin by asking yourself:

- **What are people afraid of?** During organizational change, common fears include the fear of losing one's job, fear that one's value to the organization or one's status will diminish, and fear of being unable to learn newly required skills fast enough.

- **Why do people feel these fears are justified?** Does the organization have a history of replacing employees *en masse* following a change? Have people been expected to learn new techniques and skills on their own as a mechanism for sorting out the sheep from the goats? Are people who have done the same job in the same way for a long time ignored or relegated to less important jobs?

- **What can the organization do to remove the causes of fear?** Actions as well as words are required here. While it's fine to announce at a company-wide meeting that layoffs are not part of the planned change, demonstrating support for people struggling with change—by offering training, coaching, mentoring or just extra time to learn new job requirements—and consistently rewarding employees who take advantage of these opportunites will go a lot farther to convince people that what you say is true.

Fear of...	Failure
Relationship to change:	There is a higher probability of failure and mistakes during change.

Actions to reduce fear:

✓ Don't punish mistakes.
✓ Encourage learning, don't criticize.
✓ When mistakes happen, don't ask "Who?".
  Ask "Why?" and "What was learned?"

Fear of...	The unknown
Relationship to change:	All significant changes cause people to face some element of the unknown.

Actions to reduce fear:

✓ Normalize the unknown.
✓ Communicate everything that is known.
✓ Acknowledge that it's OK not to know.
✓ Make it permissible to question anything.

Fear of...	Loss of control
Relationship to change:	Predictability always diminishes during change.

Actions to reduce fear:

✓ Involve people in the design of their new environments.
✓ Let them own the "how".

Fear of...	Job loss
Relationship to change:	Often occurs in large-scale change.

Actions to reduce fear:

✓ Be honest with people.
✓ Describe what is expected.
✓ Don't make promises you can't keep.
✓ Plan ahead to minimize job loss (e.g., increase sales to absorb productivity improvements).

Fear of...	Loss of belonging, acceptance
Relationship to change:	People may become isolated by a change and separated from the mainstream.

Actions to reduce fear:

✓ Involve, involve, involve!
✓ Use teams.
✓ Hold town meetings, think community!
✓ Create new rituals.
✓ Find time to socialize and celebrate.
✓ Share positive humor.
✓ Spread optimism.
✓ Recognize individual and group contributions.

Fear of...	Loss of competency
Relationship to change:	Those who are really good at their old jobs will undoubtedly fear this.

Actions to reduce fear:

✓ Identify what must be let go and what can be carried forward.
✓ Identify things that will stay the same.
✓ Encourage learning and have patience with those who struggle.

Fear of...	**Loss of status or peer esteem**
Relationship to change:	Present in any change involving restructuring. Often a factor in other changes as well.

Actions to reduce fear:

✓ Build opportunities for peer esteem, recognition, and status into the new environment.
✓ Honor those who contributed to past successes and help them understand how they can contribute in the new environment.

Fear of...	**Loss of organizational role**
Relationship to change:	During change this can be a reality or a false perception.

Actions to reduce fear:

✓ Identify new roles of value for those affected and coach them through the transition.
✓ Clearly communicate which roles are **not** changing.

7 Don't Wait For Perfection

*The pursuit of perfection often impedes
improvement.*

~ George F. Will

THERE is a tendency in organizations to wait for things to be just right before moving forward. There is usually no benefit and often a penalty in waiting. Delay sometimes stems from fear of the unknown and the hope that time will allow us to figure out what the unknown has in store for us before we actually go there. This is fallacious reasoning. I used to be concerned that I couldn't foresee how continuous improvement could possibly continue. Continuous improvement continues because **action generates learning**. There is no such thing as the perfect plan, so kick the habit. My preference is to err on the side of action.

Thomas Edison said, "I am not discouraged because every wrong attempt discarded is another step forward." This statement reminds us that failed attempts often provide useful information and breakthrough learning. Certainly we want to take measured risks, but many organizations seem to expect major systemic change to be implemented without a hiccup. This is clearly an unrealistic expectation. Current corporate paradigms entreat leaders to take risks while at the same time expecting them to achieve a perfect batting record. With this expectation, only the lucky survive. If you need to learn to do a triple axel, make sure you and the people who sponsor you know that you'll probably fall down a few times before you get it right.

Fear of failure drives conservatism. Conservatism drives a tentative approach that frequently translates into undershooting the goal. Mario Andretti summed it up well when he said, "If everything seems under control, you're not going fast enough." Andretti knows that to win he must push himself to the edge of being out of control. This is difficult but necessary territory for corporate leaders to travel. Develop tolerance for ambiguity and not knowing the answer. Learn how to work with others to find the answer. All large systemic changes have monsters to be tamed; they come with the territory.

Einstein gave us some insight into the source of unexpected consequences when he said, "The significant problems we face today cannot be solved at the same level of thinking we were at when we created them." When we think from within the existing paradigm we are blind to some of the consequences of our plans and actions. Ability to think outside the existing paradigm is unlikely prior to the experience of implementation: seeing is believing.

Taking action early not only allows us to learn the rules of the new paradigm but also allows us to reap low-hanging fruit and other expected benefits earlier.

Would we rather have 80% of the anticipated cost savings for a year or 100% of the savings for three months? Those who advocate the work of Pareto would suggest that 80% of the improvement can be realized with 20% of the change.

Getting A Jump On Change

A metal products fabricator was working on the implementation of cellular manufacturing. The team, composed of five people performing manual operations, had a goal to produce their product from start to finish with a batch size of one. This was quite a change from their average batch size of 300 units and a shipping quantity of 75 units per pallet. Since production lots were moved and placed on pallet racks between operations, lead times were long and inventory was stacked everywhere.

Based on the team's design, one operation required the addition of a band saw which had been ordered but was not due to arrive for eight weeks.

On my next visit we reviewed the action item list from the previous meeting. In two weeks little had progressed. They were waiting for the band saw to arrive and be tested and installed before moving forward with implementation of the perfect plan. I asked,

> *"Isn't there anything you can do to start trying the new process?"*
>
> *After much discussion the team decided that they could reduce batch size to one skid at a time, walk ten feet to the old saw until the new one arrived, and make fewer units before moving them on to the next operation. Everyone tentatively agreed that output and lead time would be better than leaving things the way they were.*
>
> *In a few days everything was ready and the new system was piloted. Products that normally took two weeks or more to get to finished goods were arriving fully painted, labeled, and packed on pallets within hours. They had captured more than 80% of the benefit of the new system weeks before the perfect plan was scheduled to begin.*

While procrastination in the name of perfection is problematic, rigidity in an implementation plan can be devastating. During change, **flexibility is essential.** It's virtually impossible to develop the perfect plan when you are exploring new territory. Anticipating the exact sequence of events can be little more than soothsaying when you're headed for uncharted waters. Plans need to be revised as new information comes to light.

This doesn't mean that constant schedule slippage is acceptable or that necessary outcomes can be compromised. It is important that targeted outcomes be maintained, which may be impossible without changing the plan. In systemic change the outcome must take priority over the plan.

When the plan is changed, be sure to communicate both the changes and the reasons to everyone affected. In most organizations the prevailing perception is that plans should be completed and remain fixed. Changing the plan is often considered a failure. This paradigm needs updating; success or failure must be contingent on achieving the envisioned outcomes, not simply rigid conformance to the plan. **Pursue perfection, don't wait for it!**

> *Before a battle, planning is everything;*
> *but during a battle, planning is useless.*
> *~ Dwight D. Eisenhower*

Questions To Ponder

? What can we do to get the new process started?

? What are the primary and secondary objectives of the change? How many can we achieve with a less than perfect plan?

? What are the potential benefits and risks in not waiting? How much improvement will waiting buy us?

? What is the simplest way to begin the change?

? If the plan calls for using a computer, how might we accomplish the objective if we didn't have one? Can we begin with a manual system to try it out before automating?

Putting The Principle Into Practice

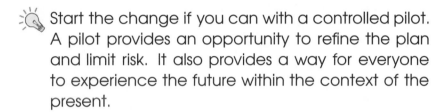 Start the change if you can with a controlled pilot. A pilot provides an opportunity to refine the plan and limit risk. It also provides a way for everyone to experience the future within the context of the present.

It's natural for people to stall or procrastinate during change. Try to implement pieces of the future plan within the current environment. If the future plan includes collecting data on a white board, why not try it out now?

Whenever the opportunity presents itself, ask which of the ideas discussed can be started right away. Using an action item list helps to ensure that there is a responsible party and an expected completion date assigned to every item.

If the plan will have to wait for something that takes substantial time, try to identify another way to continue the implementation. For example, if bar coding is suggested to eliminate transposition errors on shipping confirmation reports, consider using peel-and-stick printed labels until the bar coding can be implemented.

Keep it simple!

Making Change Stick

8 Communicate Intentionally

You can't not communicate. Everything you say and do or don't say and don't do sends a message to others.

~ John Woods

WHEN I was a plant manager for a Fortune 50 corporation, climate surveys were a way of life for determining how we were performing as leaders in the eyes of our organization. I remember feeling a bit disappointed when the first survey came back with rave reviews in every area except communication. We dutifully pursued corrective action and applied our best thinking to shore up communication—and hopefully our future score.

Two years later the experience was repeated with little improvement. Again we responded by increasing the frequency and intensity of our communication efforts. On the third survey, communication was still the biggest issue—but now "too many meetings" appeared on the list of problems!

I must admit to becoming quite frustrated over this outcome. I rationalized that apparently everyone wanted to know everything, which just isn't possible in business. Clearly there was an expectation in the minds of the workers that we were unable to understand or satisfy.

Since that time I've worked with hundreds of organizations and haven't found a single one in which people didn't rate communication as a key problem. When I ask people to identify issues that are preventing them from moving forward, they invariably say, "The trouble with our organization is that we don't communicate."

The classical pyramid structure of many organizations contributes to the problem; it encourages top-down telling rather than listening and isolates people by function. Additionally, fear tends to encourage information hoarding and the belief that sharing information diminishes individual importance and security.

> *If you don't give people information, they'll make up something to fill the void.* ~ *Carla O'Dell*

Organizational change creates unique opportunities for communication debacles. The expectation that change will fail is so strong in many organizations that it's common for people in one part of the company to declare the program D.O.A. while elsewhere it's alive and well. People feel that if they don't see anything happening in their own corner of the world, then nothing is happening anywhere.

To help avoid this problem I recommend the establishment of a communication team that represents a diagonal slice of the organization. The team is chartered to encourage wide dissemination of information and provide creative vehicles for information reconnaissance. Broad representation on the team helps to keep all areas and levels of the organization connected.

Vote Early, Vote Often!

Communicate using as many different approaches, techniques, and media as possible. Newsletters, bulletin boards, meetings, management updates, measurements, etc. are all possible methods for keeping people plugged in to what's going on. Try to make people feel that they are surrounded by and engulfed in action. Be aware, however, that you must frequently update whatever vehicles you use. If the information on your bulletin board has been stagnant for more than a few weeks, don't be surprised to hear a rumor that the patient has died. It happens that quickly!

During the stress of change, people don't always listen carefully or read thoroughly or remember things very well. For these reasons it's essential to repeat and repeat important change information. Don't assume because you've told them once or twice that they've assimilated it. Make an effort to communicate with simplified language and concentrate on only a few concepts at a time.

The grapevine is the fastest and most active communication channel in any organization. If you don't think so, spend a little time around the water cooler and you'll experience an epiphany. The grapevine can do a lot to affect the stickiness of change. If the grapevine is carrying erroneous data there is nothing wrong with interceding by feeding it more accurate information. There's nothing illegal about using this medium to your advantage!

People extract meaning from what they see as well as what they hear. It's essential to make sure that leadership's actions and words are congruent. During change it is also important to anticipate misunderstandings. In organizations with low trust levels, communication sometimes deteriorates because individuals attribute incorrect meaning to what they see and hear.

Some leaders have told me that misperception by those they lead is not their problem. **If you want to make change stick, you must accept perception management as part of your job.**

> *The most powerful communication isn't what you say, it's what you do.*   ~ *Frank E. Fischer*

Oops!

I remember a corporate quality program that espoused "doing things right the first time." We had training classes, banners, and mugs, all geared toward the elimination of rework. It was an extensive program that asked for a lot of extra effort from the workers in our factory.

All was proceeding well until a supplier shipment arrived late and out of specification. Our customers were unhappy and screaming for the parts. Since customer satisfaction was paramount to our business, we decided to rework the parts in-house instead of returning them to the supplier.

At that point mutiny broke out on the shop floor. The rallying cry was, "Why do we have to do things right the first time if the suppliers don't? Management is talking out of both sides of their mouth."

We failed to communicate why we decided to rework the parts or that we had put the supplier on "last chance" probation and charged them for the repairs. Leadership had acted responsibly but our actions had been misinterpreted. Anticipation of the misperception and a dose of preemptive communication would have avoided the setback.

Watch Your Language!

Language has a profound impact on how we think about and experience change. We need to manage our metaphors and become more conscious of their effect on our organizations and ourselves. For example, in the land of metaphor *up* is usually good and *down* usually denotes something undesirable. So expressions like "The ship is sinking", "Business is falling off", and "Sales are down" may have a more crushing impact on our psyches than we realize.

Metaphors are so ubiquitous that we often use them without thinking about them. We need to make our metaphors more intentional. Listen and try to identify them, especially from the lips of those resilient, pro-active, positive people we talked about earlier. They can teach us how to get back (up!) on our feet.

Language plays a critical role in our own self-talk and our communication with others. We have within ourselves the power to reframe how we see things. We can help others reframe by choosing our metaphors carefully and asking insightful questions.

Language also has the power to include and exclude. New terms, acronyms, and expressions often tag along with change. People in the organization who haven't learned the new buzzwords frequently feel alienated when early adopters start using these terms in conversation. Imagine yourself at a comedy club where everyone is laughing at a punch line delivered in a language you don't understand. Pay attention to the new words creeping into the organizational dialect and people's reactions when they hear them. Don't be surprised if people who feel left out and hurt start cooking up their own definitions laced with sarcasm. Capitalize on the inclusiveness of language by teaching the new terms to everyone early in the change process. If there is a large number of new words and expressions, it may even make sense to create and distribute a written glossary of terms.

Questions To Ponder

? How do people find out what is changing and what is going to change? How often is this information updated?

? Are there sources of conflicting information? Do people ask for clarification when they receive conflicting information or information they don't fully understand? If not, how can I encourage people to ask questions?

? Does everyone reporting to me understand how his job and the work of our department will be affected by the change?

? Is the change understood in other organizational functions that are essential to the operation of my department? If not, what can I do to help?

? Are there any actions we are taking that could be perceived as inconsistent with the change? If so, how can I help set the record straight?

? What is the grapevine saying? Is it accurate or inaccurate? How is it affecting the change initiative?

? Is a dynamic communication plan an integral part of our implementation planning? How can we determine the effectiveness of our change communications?

Putting The Principle Into Practice

 Don't assume that anyone understands. Always err on the side of over-communication.

Individuals have a variety of learning styles such as auditory, visual, or kinesthetic. Use as many methods and media as possible when you communicate to capture different styles.

Involve people not only in doing things themselves but also in teaching others about the change.

Make a communication plan a part of all implementation activities. Begin by asking, "What do we want people to know and how do we want them to feel after this communication?" Test your plan against the goal to ensure that it will be effective. Consider how you will determine whether the communication was successful.

Think about possible ways that people may misperceive actions and develop plans to limit negative impacts.

Tap into the grapevine.

Remember to **be the change!** If your actions aren't consistent with your words, your communication will be ineffective and the change is unlikely to stick.

Making Change Stick

9 Set People Up For Success

*Our great mistake is to try to extract from
each person virtues which he does not possess,
neglecting the cultivation of those which he
does have.*

~ Hadrian

TALENT has become the key concern of organizations and is likely to remain so for many years to come. As Jim Collins asked in his landmark book *Good To Great* [8], "What are the key seats on my bus? Do I have the right people on the bus and the right people in the right seats?" It is essential to identify the roles that are critical to implementing and sustaining change and to understand the strengths and limitations of the individuals in those roles.

Peter Drucker suggests that most leaders are batting only .333 in their ability to hire people who are the right choice for the job. Too often the hiring process becomes a personality contest more influenced by bias than objectivity. The cliché "We hire for skills and fire for attitude" strikes a resonant chord with most leaders. It may be catchy, but it's exactly backwards.

For success, attitude is equally important as ability.
~ Walter Scott

In today's turbulent marketplace, with knowledge doubling every four years, it's safe to assume that the skills required today will soon be replaced by ones we have yet to imagine. With this kind of change on the horizon we need to focus less on skills and more on attitude and aptitude.

It is essential to appreciate how attitudes and behaviors affect both individual and organizational success. With job skill requirements changing so rapidly, aptitude—the capacity and motivation to learn new things—will emerge as a key characteristic of the future workforce.

> *In a time of drastic change it is the learners who inherit the future. The learned usually find themselves equipped to live in a world that no longer exists.* ~ *Eric Hoffer*

Concurrent with a need for avid learners, a demographic shift has resulted in an increasingly diverse workforce in the United States. Diversity is a double-edged sword with conflict on one edge and synergy on the other. To be ultimately adaptable in the global marketplace, leaders must learn how to minimize conflict and maximize synergy. The need to collaborate will escalate as decision-making moves closer to the front line of customer interface.

If we believe that attitude and aptitude are critical to success, the essential question is: *How do we evaluate individuals to match them more effectively with the requirements of the job?*

There has been a lot of interest in this question over the last few years. Some organizations have defined job competencies in an effort to understand the broader behavioral spectrum of a particular job's requirements. While an appropriate endeavor, the process can become problematic when we attempt to compare individuals against the competencies in an objective manner.

Analytical tools are commercially available that use a more generalized approach to synthesize behavioral, motivational, and capability benchmarks for organizational positions. These assessments further provide a statistically valid way of evaluating individuals with respect to the benchmarks.

I have helped several of my clients complete job benchmarks using these tools and feel that benchmarking can significantly augment the existing placement process. These assessments can quantitatively identify characteristics that are difficult to ascertain or measure during an interview. They also provide insights for interview exploration into areas that might otherwise go unnoticed until they manifest themselves as a "poor fit" between an individual and a job or organization. In virtually all the jobs we have benchmarked there have been measurable improvements in both on-the-job performance and talent retention.

The same types of analytical tools can be used for reassignment within an organization or for personal development of individuals currently holding a position. The ability to evaluate individuals with respect to the characteristics needed for outstanding performance in a job provides a measurable path for improvement.

Job requirements must be dictated by what the job actually requires, not by intuitive notions of what kind of person can do the job or has done the job in the past. In other words, what characteristics does this job need in order to deliver superior measurable performance? Try not to fall into the trap of personalizing the job analysis based on the people who are currently in the position. Even current top performers may not be functioning at the maximum potential of the job.

In benchmarking the field sales force of a large and successful company, I found that the top performers in the job displayed behavioral styles that were naturally introverted. These people became successful in their jobs because of their motivational preference rather than their behavioral style; they modified their behavior to fit the requirements of a high-contact "people" job.

The job itself would seem to require a different natural behavioral style if we failed to take into account the ability of highly motivated workers to adapt their behavior to the needs of the job.

Change frequently requires the redeployment of people and the reassignment of tasks. The research of Dr. Kevin D. Gazzara of Intel Corporation has determined that people's job satisfaction is related to how closely the proportion of routine, project, and troubleshooting tasks in their job matches their personal preference. Dr. Gazzara has developed an assessment to quantify the job, individual, and optimized proportions of these task types. Tools of this kind can help individuals find more job satisfaction, which is intimately connected to higher levels of commitment and achievement.

Capitalizing on strengths is a rapid and effective way to build competency and confidence. It's much easier for people to excel when they are drawing on strong natural abilities.

> *The hard stuff is easy. It's the soft stuff that's hard.*
> *~ Fred Smith*

It's important to help individuals find a seat on the organizational bus that resonates with them. Often this requires identifying and understanding a person's natural talents. Howard Gardner's research regarding multiple intelligences gives us insight into the variety of unique natural strengths that individuals can exhibit.

Daniel Goleman's groundbreaking book *Emotional Intelligence* [9] dovetails with Gardner's work and helps us understand why a high IQ alone doesn't guarantee success in a world highly dependent on interpersonal relationships. Emotional intelligence is the capacity for recognizing our own feelings and those of others (empathy). It includes the ability to manage our own emotions and to influence, persuade, and assist others. Don't ignore emotional intelligence. Cultivate it in everyone, and particularly in leaders.

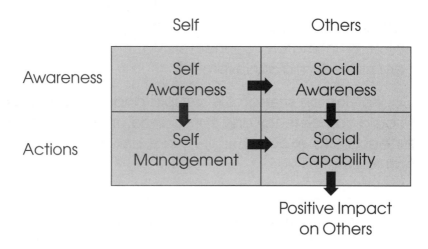

Figure 9.1. Emotional Intelligence

I have a simple theory about people and jobs: **people who are passionate about their jobs will outperform those who are not... every time**. Even if a person is exceptionally talented and has a behavioral style that fits perfectly with a given career, nothing will happen if there is no inspiration. Passion is the fire in the boiler. Passion can be unlocked when the source of an individual's enthusiasm is discovered and invited into service.

Stacking The Deck

I worked as a production superintendent for a company that had the policy of promoting from within. I conducted many interviews of existing employees who wanted new positions but did not have the skills needed to be successful. They all expected to get the job because of their records as good employees.

After dealing with several disappointed job seekers, I began encouraging people to stack the deck in their favor. I asked people to put themselves in my position. How would they decide who should get the job when five equally great employees apply? What could they do to guarantee that I would pick them?

Following these conversations, two employees took it upon themselves to enroll in the local community college and complete courses in machining, which was an area that we were expanding. Both ultimately became journeyman machinists.

Questions To Ponder

? Do I believe that a key role of leadership is to help people to grow?

? What are the strengths and weaknesses of the people who report to me?

? Are the people in my department in positions that optimize their strengths and minimize their weaknesses?

? Is there clear and accurate documentation of the skill and behavioral requirements for every position in my department, particularly those affected by the change?

? Do we have formal job benchmarks for critical positions? Other positions?

? Are the metrics used to assess job performance understood by everyone?

? If I will hire new people to accommodate the change, how will I determine their behavioral styles, aptitudes, motivators, and work preferences?

? Is everyone in my department aware of new positions that may be opening or positions whose responsibilities will change?

? If job tasks are changing, who will participate in defining the new tasks?

? What opportunities can we offer to employees who would like their jobs to be different?

? Are there people in my department who seem particularly frustrated in their work or unsuited to the jobs they are doing now? What can we do to change the situation for them?

Putting The Principle Into Practice

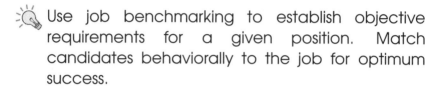 Use job benchmarking to establish objective requirements for a given position. Match candidates behaviorally to the job for optimum success.

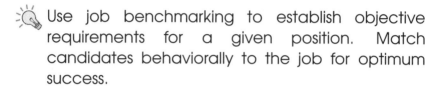 Within the boundaries of necessary outcomes, allow people to decide how to do their jobs. People are most successful when they can execute their job in harmony with their own personal style.

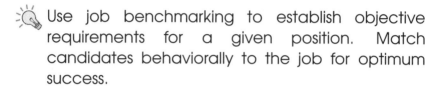 Determine people's talents and use them.

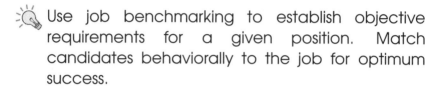 Focus on people's strengths.

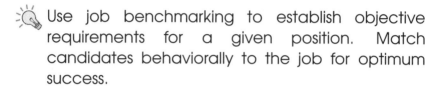 Try to make jobs congruent with task preferences (i.e., routine, project, problem-solving).

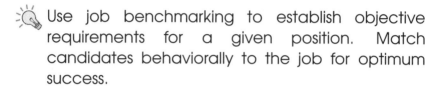 Coach others to be more successful in their positions. Find out what people love about their jobs. Encourage people to cultivate their Emotional Intelligence.

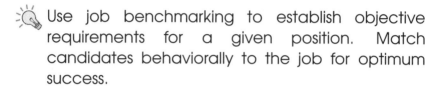 Determine what frustrates people about their jobs and make every effort to remove the source of frustration. This may be accomplished by direct intervention or by helping people reframe their view of the situation.

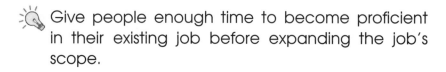 Give people enough time to become proficient in their existing job before expanding the job's scope.

Take time to talk to people about their current position and their aspirations.

Making Change Stick

10

Catch People Doing Something Right

We increase whatever we praise.

~ Charles Fillmore

IMAGINE trying to get an infant to take her first step the same way we try to get people to take on new behaviors during change at work. The conventional management approach involves leaning over the crib to inform the baby that next Tuesday she is scheduled to take her first step. Mommy and Daddy describe how they are counting on her and remind her that she's had months to prepare by watching all those other people walk. She is told that Mommy and Daddy do not expect her to have a problem. A procedure on how to walk is placed in the crib, she's encouraged to go for it and reminded to let Mommy know how she does.

This approach obviously would be a formula for disaster. In contrast, most parents carefully watch for their child to demonstrate something that vaguely resembles the new desired behavior. Even the slightest move in the right direction is met with praise and excited phone calls to Grandma and Grandpa.

The same approach works equally well with children in big bodies. Change would stick a lot better if we treated adults adapting to change the same way we pay attention to and encourage an infant learning to walk.

Most organizations in transition focus their efforts on "fixing" the people who aren't getting it. Those who seem to be doing all right are left to their own devices. While this is conventional wisdom, it doesn't do much to create a critical mass of people who are exhibiting the desired new behaviors. While it's certainly important to help people who are having difficulty making the change, we must not overlook the importance of recognizing, acknowledging, and encouraging those who are trying their best to embrace it.

At the same time, we need to be cognizant of not rewarding contradictory behaviors associated with the old rules.

The Arsonist Fireman

I worked with a medical equipment manufacturer suffering from poor delivery performance on their main product line. They were losing much of their business to overseas providers and the customer service department was at their wits' end trying to placate irate customers.

After some analysis we conceived of a cellular manufacturing process and a production planning system that would alleviate the problem. The changes were implemented quickly. Within weeks the backorder problem was resolved and the complaint phone in customer service was quiet.

A month or two later when I visited the client I found that backorders were beginning to occur again in the product line we had fixed. Following a brief tour of the shop, I asked when the fabrication cell had become a ghost town. John, the supervisor, informed me that he'd had to reassign the workers to another area this week because of a crisis. We got all of the people back to their assigned cell only to have the same situation repeat itself every few months.

The president of the company was calling for John's head. It wasn't until I asked why John would repeatedly break what we had already fixed that we began to understand the dynamics of the situation.

Prior to the change John was the company's most valuable player. Whenever customer service had a really angry customer ready to cancel an order they would call John and he would jump to allocate resources to put out the fire. John regularly received accolades from customer service as he saved the day. John also received a big fat bonus at the end of the year for his ability to respond to customer emergencies (regardless of who created them). John was great at putting out fires.

I don't think that John was acting maliciously. He was just doing what he had always been rewarded for. He was responding to a rule that had worked for him for years: move the resources from the areas where you don't have a problem to the area where you do have a problem.

I'm fairly sure that John was also quite disturbed by the change in procedure. It was clear that before long fires would be eliminated. How important will the fireman be if there are no fires?

Supervisors are often the hardest hit by changes since they have a long history of heroically holding the company together by working around systemic problems in their areas. When the long-standing problems are finally eliminated, it's natural for them to fear that their value to the company will be reduced. But what is really happening (if it's done right) is a role shift from expediter to facilitator.

It's important to acknowledge the particularly difficult transition of the individuals most affected by the change. Help people through their role changes and try to appreciate and communicate their continued value and importance to the organization.

We cannot change others; we can only influence others to change themselves. Even our most diligent efforts are sometimes ineffective for individuals stuck in a dysfunctional state outside acceptable boundaries. Resistance in the form of foot dragging is one thing, outright sabotage is another. Sabotage must be dealt with swiftly. There is also a limit to how much time can responsibly be spent supporting the few individuals lagging through transition.

People who are honestly struggling and trying to get through the transition merit support more than those who refuse to move forward. Those who are unable or unwilling to assimilate the change must be confronted in such a way that the consequences of their resistance are clearly understood. They need to know how they are affecting their future and the future of the other stakeholders in the organization. As always, we must communicate respectfully. Expectations should be clearly expressed in as open and safe an environment as possible.

Leaders shouldn't have to bear the sole responsibility for recognition. Peers see us all day long; when a person who sees us on good days and bad days catches us doing something right, it's truly meaningful. Inviting everyone to participate in giving recognition allows the criteria for recognition to become well known and firmly embedded in the culture.

Recognizing Excellence

I worked with one of my clients to develop a peer-level reward system called the "A2A" (Associate-to-Associate) program. Our first action was to identify behaviors that would take the organization closer to achieving their vision. The team assigned to create the system polled the organization for ideas and then brainstormed a number of likely behaviors. These behaviors were voted on by the organization to select the top ten. An A2A form was created that documented the behaviors and rules established for the award.

Anyone in the organization could give any other associate the award if that person displayed any of the ten behaviors in an extraordinary way. The form has a location to note specifically what the individual did and nine pre-printed check boxes to allow the award giver to check off the appropriate behaviors. The A2A program itself covered the tenth behavior, which was described as "Gives recognition for the efforts of other associates."

The A2A form, available to everyone, is submitted and posted on the bulletin board in the cafeteria for a month. At company-wide meetings, the president reads the forms aloud and awards each recipient a personalized certificate of appreciation while the rest of the company applauds and cheers. Many recipients proudly display the certificates in their work areas.

After seeing the program in action, the president demonstrated his trust in people's ability to recognize excellence in their peers by contributing a $25 gift certificate to accompany every award. The system has been in place for over a decade and continues to be a good way to recognize people for doing the right thing.

Questions To Ponder

? What behaviors should I be looking for?

? What is the best way for me to show my appreciation? How might others perceive my way?

? Am I acknowledging the appropriate behaviors? Are my observations accurate?

? Do I need praise? If not, how can I be aware of the need of others for acknowledgment? How do I feel about that need?

? Am I comfortable giving praise?

Putting The Principle Into Practice

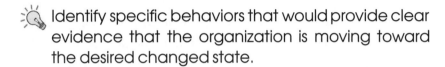 Identify specific behaviors that would provide clear evidence that the organization is moving toward the desired changed state.

Recognize small steps toward the goal. For example, if you are trying to improve quality, take notice of the first day or the first week without any defects. Affirm that people are heading in the right direction.

Any system of recognition needs to be accurate. Pay attention to ensure that only those exhibiting the desired behaviors are rewarded. The goal is to recognize as many people as possible doing the right thing. In this case it's not an exclusive contest to find one individual who is best but rather an inclusive opportunity for everybody to "win".

Consider developing a system that allows individuals to nominate their peers for recognition. Peer recognition is frequently the most effective means of motivating change.

Avoid generalizations when giving feedback. When appreciation is communicated it should be specific to the behavior that you want repeated.

For example, if you tell people that they did a great job on their report it may be difficult for them to know what characteristics of the report you liked. If you say instead that you really liked the way they analyzed the data and graphed the results, they have specific information about how to replicate the performance in the future.

11 Measure Stuff That Matters

If you cannot measure it, you cannot improve it.

~ Lord Kelvin

THE mantra for measurements should be **focused, few, frequent**, and **followed**. Large systemic changes are undertaken to address key strategic business concerns. Measurements should be selected that track how the organization is performing against whatever business parameter best reflects those concerns. If delivery performance is an issue, measuring the percentage of orders shipped on time is an appropriate choice. Pay strict attention to the details of what is being measured and how, since numbers can be massaged into a "feel good" form.

One of my clients had documented near perfect on-time delivery concurrent with massive numbers of delivery complaints from irate customers. The paradox was unraveled when we found that the on-time measurement was based on a company commitment date rather than the customer's requested delivery date. The company always delivered on its twelve-week promise to the customer who wanted the goods in three.

Start Now!

Initiating measurements is always a bit rugged. Measurement accuracy will improve as the nuances of each measurement are refined. Listen carefully but try to resist diluting the measurement when people complain that it's unfair because of one or more exceptions to the rule that they can't control. Above all, don't delay in beginning to measure because you can't achieve 100% accuracy. Most measurements will be accurate enough to see whether improvement is occurring or not.

> *Don't take action if you have only enough information to give you less than a 40 percent chance of being right, but don't wait until you have enough facts to be 100 percent sure, because by then it is almost always too late.*
> *~ General Colin Powell*

You can begin with a crayon in the shipping department; it's quick to implement and works just fine. Simple is better, so avoid getting hung up waiting for complex modifications to programs or reports from your ERP system. Yes, bar coding might be nice but it's not essential and it could delay or complicate your project.

Expect to encounter resistance to measurement. In some organizations fear of mistakes has created a "smoke and mirrors" culture. This ostrich-like approach asserts that if nothing is measured then no one can be singled out for blame. Hitting a target blindfolded is a matter of chance: measurement is essential to making predictable improvements. Be careful, however, not to escalate fear and resistance by publicly measuring individuals against one another. If you have fear of mistakes or a witch-hunting style of problem solving in your organization, deal with those issues first to ensure that the measurements you implement will be accurate and effective.

Why Not Now?

A small printing company was losing customers because their delivery lead times were too long. Curiously, they weren't even measuring delivery performance when I arrived. I was perplexed, especially when I asked how their delivery was and they responded, "Good."

We discussed how they could begin measuring on-time shipment to customer expectation. Resistance flared as the production planner insisted that delivery was not in their control. He insisted that the customers never approved their proofs on time and besides the customers don't understand how hard it is to do this job.

Idea after idea on how to measure was proposed and shot down by the team. There was no computer report available, they didn't have bar coding, they didn't know when the customer wanted it and were afraid to ask. With many possibilities eliminated, they figured that if they started working on a plan the measurement could probably be implemented in 6 to 12 months.

Finally in frustration I drew a large table with three columns: **Date / On Time / Late**. *I asked, "How about we start measuring on time to promise in the shipping department by recording hash marks on this chart every day and see how it goes?"*

The group ultimately agreed to give it a go. They said they could start in a few weeks. I asked, "Why not tomorrow?" No one could come up with a good reason. And so it began the very next day.

Sometimes Less Is More

Try to resist measuring too many things. Local measurements may be needed to diagnose and solve problems, but global change should be evaluated by a handful of key strategic measures. These measurements should be produced on a regular basis without fail, posted for all to see, and regularly discussed. Don't let small numbers scare you; the absolute measurement is not nearly as important as the trend. When customer service wants to stop measuring because they're depressed about the 14% on-time shipment metric, ask what can be done to make it 20%.

The frequency of measurement should be appropriate to what is being measured. Balance the need for feedback with the burden of collection. For key top-level metrics, aggregating data into weekly and monthly buckets seems to be a good compromise between adequate reinforcement and excessive nervousness. Keep building on previous data so everyone can easily see the direction and rate of change. The fewer the measurements, the easier it will be to keep people focused on the important issues.

I'm a strong advocate of simple graphics. Plot the numbers with bar graphs, pie charts, or line graphs and resist adding so much data that you have to run a course in graph reading before people can understand what they're seeing.

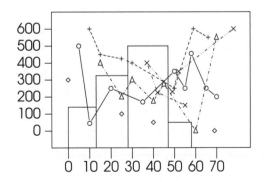

You Have To Do It To Use It

It's extremely important that the measurements be maintained. People really want to know what's important to focus on, particularly during change. Will people think it's important to reduce inventory levels if the inventory graph hasn't been updated for 6 weeks and nobody's heard a peep from management? Not likely, especially when every day at least 3 or 4 people ask them how many units they've produced so far.

People will pay attention to what leadership pays attention to; it's a survival strategy. For the most part people are still conditioned to the command and control structure; many would like someone to tell them what's important. When everything seems to be somebody's top priority, most people are looking for a sign to help them distinguish the essential from the non-essential.

But beware of the propensity for either/or thinking, which manifests itself in inversely proportional relationships. For example, many people will tell you that higher production quotas will result in decreased quality. While there may be some truth to this argument, it's mostly based on how things have unfolded in the past. The right question in this case would be to ask what would have to change for daily output to go up and quality defects to be reduced at the same time. "If we wanted to double output and reduce defects, what would have to be different?"

Some key business measures truly are inversely related. You may need to select two related measures to avoid deluding yourself with a false sense of euphoria. In the case of on-time shipment, you should also measure inventory. As an operations manager, I used to claim that operations managers were heroes only during the 30 seconds between going off backorder with the customer and the accounting department's noticing that there was too much inventory.

Remember to measure the **few** things that keep your organization's attention **focused** on the bigger change. Keep score **frequently** enough to both motivate and detect trends, and be sure to publicly **follow** results with course corrections or, hopefully, celebrations.

> *Make measurable progress in reasonable time.*
> ~ *Jim Rohn*

When the tail wagging the dog is a good thing!

As a part of creating a focused factory and self-directed work teams, we established measurement goals for every team. Each team had a goal to improve on-time shipments, inventory turns, productivity/cost, quality, and safety. It wasn't long before a friendly competition developed among the teams to see who could achieve the best on-time shipment number.

On-time shipment was a daily measurement that I would publish by 10:00 each morning for every team. It was a zero-tolerance measurement that required the entire order to ship on the date requested by the customer or no credit was given.

It was about 10 minutes past 10 o'clock when two machine operators accosted me outside my office asking the whereabouts of the numbers. At first I was taken back and a little angry that they were demanding the numbers and holding me accountable to be on time to the minute. But when I reflected on the event I realized that having line people take that much interest in the business was nothing short of miraculous. My wish had actually come true.

The teams went on to have the IT department develop a daily report that told them specifically what parts of an order didn't get shipped. Tracking was also provided so causal information could be collected to help create effective corrective action.

I remember having to contain myself from chuckling when the director of customer service called with her nose out of joint because she had been grilled by some hourly production folks. They wanted to know why their products hadn't shipped when they had made it to finished goods with time to spare. They were correct! Because of their questions we detected a program glitch in our ERP software and corrected it. In the old environment that glitch was well under the radar and would never have been found. **Things that get measured have a tendency to get better.**

Questions To Ponder

? Might the selected measurement drive an undesirable outcome elsewhere? If so, is there another measurement that can minimize the negative effect?

? Does the measurement tie directly to a strategic objective? If so, which one(s)?

? Do individuals understand how their work affects the measurement?

? Are goals clearly established for each measurement?

? How do I react when a metric is negatively trending? Positively trending?

? When was the last time I looked at the metrics? When was the last time I discussed them with someone else?

Putting The Principle Into Practice

Keep the 80/20 rule in mind. It is likely that 80% of the improvement can be captured with 20% of the implementation effort.

If fear is making people reluctant to attempt the change, start small. Ask what it would take to begin the change and achieve *some* improvement over the current method.

Gain agreement on the concept first, then solicit creative ways to implement it. "Since we all agree that it's important to minimize carrying of product, what could we do to get closer to that goal?"

Select only a handful of strategically significant measurements to track. If the measurements are not significant to the stakeholders, consider different measurements. Start with customer satisfaction.

Select a time period that makes sense for detection of change without over-reaction to normal variation. A correction in response to normal variation often makes matters worse. Look for trends and abnormal swings.

Be prompt in updating measurements. Eliminate measurements that you are unwilling or unable to keep up with.

Maintain history and graph trends (e.g., 3 month rolling average). Keep graphs as visual and simple as possible.

 Make sure that individuals can tie their personal work actions to specific measurements.

 Don't wait for the perfect measurement to start. Measurement accuracy gets better only through the process of measurement. Set interim goals that can be achieved while the measurement is being refined.

 A functioning model of the change will accelerate the process. Suggest that pilot experiments be done to test ideas. Some people have to see it—or do it—to believe it.

 Personal computers didn't arrive on the scene until the 1980's, yet people managed to measure things long before that. Before jumping to high tech solutions, try the simple ones.

 Much of the information collected in organizations today is needed because the system is complex. If you reduce the complexity of the system you can also reduce the need for information.

12 Lead From The Heart

A good head and a good heart are always a formidable combination.

~ Nelson Mandela

FOR many years people have interpreted the expression "my heart's not in it" as metaphorical. However, research by organizations such as HeartMath® has identified neurons in the heart and determined that the heart actually carries on a measurable two-way dialogue with the brain. Their research shows that messages sent by the heart to the brain can also affect performance.

The magnetic field produced by the heart is more than 5,000 times stronger than the field generated by the brain and can be detected several feet away from the body in all directions. Current research indicates that one person's heart signals can affect another's brain waves; heart-brain synchronization occurs between people when they interact. So besides being metaphorical, it may well be literally true that others can subconsciously detect the signals being broadcast by our hearts.

Behind every sticky change you are likely to find at least one key leader who is passionate about the change.

It's usually a leader who is influential and respected by a broad cross-section of the organizational community. These are leaders who "have their hearts in it." When we lead with the heart we are displaying a 100% investment of our human energy in the change. In this state we are authentic in our interactions and show genuine concern and caring for the successful transition of those around us.

> *Leadership is practiced not so much in words as in attitude and in actions.* ~ *Harold S. Geneen*

Analytical skills, however helpful in the technical components of change, need to be augmented by an understanding of the needs and concerns of human beings in transition.

It's important to view the organization as a community of people rather than just a big machine with people serving as replaceable components. A community view causes us to look deeper into the contributions made by people who have helped the organization in critical but not always obvious ways. It allows us to value each person's contribution and appreciate that resistance to change may be motivated by a desire to protect the organization from harm.

Transition is a wholly human process. Focusing on leading with the heart is intended to remind us of that fact. Do not misunderstand; this principle is not about being gullible or soft-hearted or allowing resistant people to undermine critical change. Rather, it is about acknowledging that the principles that work so well for *things* fall short when it comes to people.

People can change, but they cannot *be* changed. Interestingly, the precursor to change is frequently a "change of heart."

> *If you want to build a ship, then don't drum up men to gather wood, give orders, and divide the work. Rather, teach them to yearn for the far and endless sea.* ~ *Antoine de Saint-Exupery*

The ability to lead change effectively comes from deep inside. It involves beliefs about the change and beliefs about the people involved. ***Belief leads leaders.*** This expression captures a simple yet important concept. It's much easier to lead when we believe strongly in what we are doing. Our belief precedes our actions and guides us. Our belief helps us find the heart to move forward.

To lead with heart we have to assimilate the change and internalize it. Once we have *our* hearts in the right place we can focus on capturing and moving those around us. "Having our hearts in the right place" includes acknowledging that caring for members of the organizational community is paramount to a successful change.

While this does not mean that change will necessarily occur without casualties, it does suggest that we will deal with our wounded as respected members of the community rather than as expendable entities. The attitude of survivors in caring organizations is much different than in uncaring ones.

While leadership decisions can be painful and difficult, cutting off communication from the heart by numbing ourselves with an "it's just business" frame of mind leads to sub-optimal decisions that can derail the change. It is important to stay connected both intellectually and emotionally with the change.

We lead best when we are fully engaged with heart, mind, and body. The emergence of informal leaders in organizations is evidence of the magnetic affect of this congruence. Would you prefer to follow someone who leads with the heart? I've never had a single person answer "No" to that question. With such a unanimous response, why is it so rare for people to lead this way?

Traditional leadership culture defines successful leaders as strong-minded and heart-focused ones as weak. We need to dispel this either/or thinking and replace it with both/and:

"What would it take to lead with both strength and heart?"

"Isn't that what we really want?"

A paradigm shift is in the making!

A Shift

We were in the planning stages of a major reorganization into self-directed work teams. It was a traumatic change affecting the real and perceived status of many people in the organization. Our research indicated that we should expect fallout (notice the euphemism) of about 15% of our workforce during the change.

As we were designing our change process, that number haunted me. The 15% represented about 60 people. More disconcerting to me was that we were designing a process that tacitly accepted that number as an expected outcome.

Finally, unable to contain myself, at a team meeting I asked, "How would this process be different if we didn't want to lose any people?"

After the initial shock subsided, the team agreed that we should take some time to brainstorm the possibilities. We redesigned the process to have a target of zero lost people. About three percent of our people left the company during the change. While we didn't hit our target, we reduced the expected fallout by 80%. This was not only people-friendly, it was bottom-line business friendly—a true win-win outcome!

More important, yet more difficult to quantify, was the positive impact on everyone who went through the change. The process we designed was simply more people-sensitive. The approach we took, while initially appearing to be a longer path, actually facilitated the change. I believe our shift to lead from the heart moved many of our people to embrace the change.

Questions To Ponder

? How optimistic am I about this change?

? Do I think that the people in the organization have what it takes to implement the change? If not, where do I find them lacking? What can be done to change this?

? What can I do to build trust within the organization?

? What am I doing to increase my credibility with my reports? What else could I be doing?

? Who in the organization is passionate about the change?

? How can I balance compassion and high expectations?

Putting The Principle Into Practice

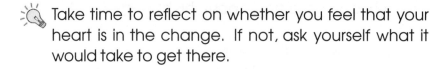 Take time to reflect on whether you feel that your heart is in the change. If not, ask yourself what it would take to get there.

Ⓠ In a difficult change you may have mixed emotions. It is important to be aware of that possibility and to recognize it as a normal reaction. Acknowledgment will enhance commitment.

Ⓠ Remember that the goal is to influence the people around you to *change themselves*.

Ⓠ Apply the golden rule: treat everyone affected by the change the way you would want to be treated.

Ⓠ Avoid gallows humor, euphemisms, and other desensitizing techniques.

Ⓠ Look for people who have their heart in it and ask them to help lead the change.

Ⓠ If saying the words *heart, community, compassion, caring* makes you uncomfortable, ask yourself why. What is the stigma associated with these words in your current culture? Try to identify the either/or model and ask what it would take to redefine it as both/and.

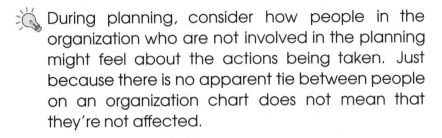 During planning, consider how people in the organization who are not involved in the planning might feel about the actions being taken. Just because there is no apparent tie between people on an organization chart does not mean that they're not affected.

Ask people how they *feel*.

Reflect on decisions and ask yourself what went well and what you could have done better.

13

Creating A Structure For Change

There are two things to be considered with regard to any scheme. In the first place, "Is it good in itself?" In the second, "Can it be easily put into practice?"

~ Jean Jacques Rousseau

THE large number of variables involved and the uniqueness of each organization preclude the creation of a precise formula for effecting sticky change. We can describe the desired result, but not the exact steps needed to get there in a particular organization—rather like a recipe that instructs you to bake bread "until golden brown" rather than specifying the number of minutes it should stay in the oven. This "in the ball park" method is sometimes the only way to provide directions that are useful in circumstances where all variables cannot be identified or controlled.

It's really hard to tell whether the bread is golden brown if the term "golden brown" isn't understood—or if no one is looking. It is important that a wise and knowledgeable guiding body be created to assess the change process along the way, make decisions, and modify the plan as needed.

Some organizations call this transformation management group a steering team. I've begun calling it the *guidance team* to avoid the image of a nightmarish ride in the back seat of a car driven by quarreling committee members. Some organizations ignore transformation management and assume that a series of training events will achieve the required outcome. While training is important, it cannot identify or correct a change initiative gone awry.

The overseeing body should be composed of key leaders as well as individuals who will be directly involved in facilitating the change. It is important to create a network of people who are viscerally connected to the transformation and charged with spreading the change throughout the organization.

Every team associated with the change process should be connected through the network to the guidance team. In large organizations this may require the assignment of executive sponsors to specific project teams to assist them in overcoming obstacles and to give team members a voice on the guidance team.

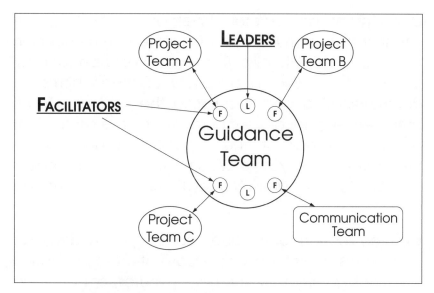

Figure 13.1. Guidance Team Network

The guidance team is responsible for educating itself, establishing goals, planning the change, measuring progress, and modifying the plan when necessary. The team must be well-informed regarding organizational resistance, cultural misalignment, morale, and performance failures.

All members of the guidance team must act in a manner consistent with the desired change. Early in the guidance team's development this subject should be discussed and appropriate behaviors identified, documented, and encouraged.

The guidance team should spawn a team whose function is organization-wide communication and motivation. This team should represent a diagonal slice of the company, with members from different departments and different levels of responsibility. The intention is to stimulate and facilitate communication up, down, and laterally. The team should be formally chartered to develop a variety of mechanisms for communicating and stimulating the change. Team members should be encouraged to represent their respective areas of the organization and to be pro-active conveyors of information. Select people carefully for this team; it is a key to making your change stick.

Communication teams often come up with ideas like newsletters, bulletin boards, state-of-the-organization meetings, posting of meeting minutes, small group meetings, photos, awards, etc. Short-circuiting this approach—implementing the same solutions without a team—isn't nearly as good as having a team develop its own plan. Team members who have a stake in communicating the change will become missionary advocates, spreading the word better than any media. Team members with credibility in their own departments have a higher probability of being trusted, listened to, and confided in.

In his book *The Tipping Point: How Little Things Can Make a Big Difference* [10], Malcolm Gladwell presented the idea of personality types that can enhance the spread of ideas. Gladwell calls people who interact with large numbers of people "Connectors" and those who have a passion for developing expertise "Mavens". If you want a new idea to become an epidemic in your organization, pollinate your communication team with Connectors and Mavens.

A word of caution. Some organizations implement a formal, up-the-pyramid communication system like a suggestion-box system. While this is inherently a noble idea, most such attempts fail. Formality creates a barrier to relationships and the feeling of community. System rigidity can set up overworked leaders for public failure if they struggle with the required follow-through. Remember, people are often concerned about change and are sensitive to subtle evidence that might support their concerns. Formal employee feedback systems can be sustained only by the prompt personal acknowledgment of individual contributions and periodic updates regarding the disposition of suggestions. How many times would you give your feedback to an organization that took weeks to get back to you?

> *Success is nothing more than a few simple disciplines, practiced every day.* ~ Jim Rohn

Most opportunities for improvement span organizational boundaries; cross-functional teams should implement these changes. People should not be arbitrarily appointed as team leaders or facilitators; instead, individuals should be carefully chosen for development in those roles. Don't assume that the skills that make a good manager or technician in your organization today ensure the ability to facilitate others into the future.

Teams, team leaders, and facilitators should be selected based on attitude and aptitude and then trained, coached and practiced. High-performing teams are composed of individuals with diverse backgrounds who have learned how to work together to **capitalize on their differences**. The potential for synergy is diminished in untrained teams that appear to come together by luck; their cohesiveness usually stems from membership similarity rather than great team process.

To emphasize the importance of the change initiative, ask project teams to present their goals, plans, and results to the guidance team at periodic intervals. This process helps keep the project moving and provides a forum for team members and key leaders to communicate.

Organizations with a large number of teams should consider establishing a *learning community* of team facilitators. Peer meetings provide an opportunity to elevate skills by sharing lessons learned and cross-pollinating teams with creative practices that work. Creating a learning community can also enhance community spirit. Time expended can be minimized and a sense of belonging fostered by holding meetings over lunch and providing time for both work and relationship development.

The guidance team should establish a budget for positively reinforcing individuals and groups that demonstrate adoption of the change. The rewards do not have to be large but they should be publicly bestowed upon those who have demonstrated the right stuff. Construct your rules to have as many legitimate award receivers as possible without diluting the message. Highly competitive contests with few winners are inappropriate for this purpose.

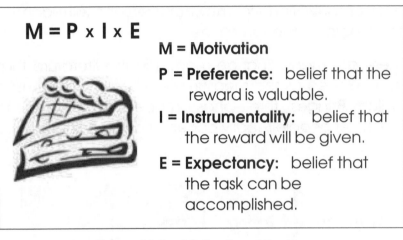

$$M = P \times I \times E$$

M = Motivation

P = Preference: belief that the reward is valuable.

I = Instrumentality: belief that the reward will be given.

E = Expectancy: belief that the task can be accomplished.

Figure 13.2. Motivational Factors

To paraphrase Victor Vroom's theory of expectation, in order to be motivated individuals must believe they can accomplish what has been asked, that they want the reward that is promised, and that if they deliver they will receive the reward. If any of the three requirements is missing there will be no motivation. So if you promise a stuffed animal to anyone who can run a four-minute mile, don't expect a lot of takers even if they're sure you'll deliver.

Remember that the organization is changing both physically and emotionally. The guidance team must monitor both processes. The physical change is easily measured using project management techniques; most organizations are quite adept at managing this aspect of change. The transition of the individuals in the organization, however, is more complex; creativity will be needed to develop a system for monitoring progress. Remember that since it is a personal as well as an organizational journey, not everyone will reach the same point at the same time.

There are many change models in the literature that can be used as the measurement scale. I have used William Bridges' three-phase model and have found that most people readily accept it as meaningful.

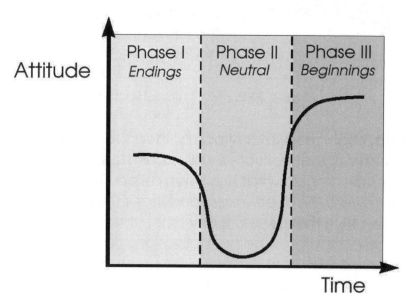

Figure 13.3. Change Curve

On a periodic basis, ask people to mark on the change curve where they think they are. Early in the change process, because of the high probability of fear, this exercise may have to be done anonymously. Using a model has the benefit of normalizing the process and creating a common understanding and language for discussing how, what, and why we are feeling.

Knowing where people are on the change curve will help in deciding what action is needed to minimize the effects of the emotional transition. It will also help to identify early implementers and provide clues about what needs to be done for whom to reduce anxiety.

14

Aristotle Got It

The whole is greater than the sum of the parts.

~ Aristotle

Final Questions To Ponder

? What aspects of the change have gone better than expected so far?

? Where have unanticipated problems arisen?

? What can we infer about how people perceive the change?

THE recipe for sticky change is not really different from a recipe for cooking a gourmet meal. All the ingredients must be used in the correct proportions appropriate to the change that your organization is cooking up. Successful change requires leadership that understands and applies all the principles and is an integral part of the process.

Great change leadership develops from the inside out. Cultivating our own adaptability and resilience is a key factor in leading change effectively. It's difficult to sell an idea that we don't believe in. Halfhearted change will not stick.

As leaders, we may sometimes be asked to implement changes that we don't agree with. These requests create the most difficult soul searching. It is important to understand what we disagree about and why. It's a good idea to reframe and look at the situation from as many different angles as possible to ensure that we are seeing the request for change and our own reactions as clearly as possible. Ask the question, "What's best for the organization?"—and, of equal importance, "What's best for me?" The best solution will optimize the needs of the organization without compromising our integrity or core beliefs.

> *People don't resist change. They resist being changed!*
>   ~ *Peter Senge*

Change is usually easier for leaders than it is for followers; it is easier to be a change initiator than a change recipient. A glaring exception occurs when the success of the change requires a cultural transformation. In this case leadership becomes the change recipient as well as the change initiator. I believe that more changes will fall into this category over the next decade as the rate of change increases. Awareness of organizational culture (Principle #4) will not eliminate this issue. However, following the principle allows a conflict between culture and change to be discovered early enough to realign the culture before undertaking the change.

Conventional leadership wisdom suggests that organizational members function in isolation. This thinking leads to the stereotypical gulf between "them" and "us". Before passing judgment that "they" just don't get it, we should consider the likelihood that their lack of understanding is connected to something that we, as leaders, don't get. It is an illusion to believe that leadership does not have a significant influence, both directly and indirectly, on the thoughts and behaviors of everyone in the organization.

Embedded within the principles of sticky change is an implied model for leadership that challenges the traditional one. It relies on leaders who have developed their emotional intelligence. A key difference from the classical model is the relationship between power and control.

Some leaders believe that in order to be powerful one must have direct control over one's environment, that power and control are intimately connected. Unfortunately, this model has finite limits based on our capacity to control and the consequences of stifling the human capacity of others working within our domain.

The sticky change principles rely on leadership that defines power as the *capacity to accomplish* and decouples it from direct control. In this model, the capacity for achievement can be increased well beyond that of any individual by relinquishing control to an ever-expanding group of competent and committed doers. Leadership in this context takes on the role of creating and propagating an environment (culture) that attracts competency and engenders commitment.

> *Relinquish control and gain power.*
>
> ~ *Rich Reale*

By now you may have noticed subtle connections between the principles that make the boundaries between them a little fuzzy. Do not be concerned; it is more important to understand the principles applied as a whole rather than as isolated entities. As an integrated whole they represent a blueprint for the creation of a more resilient and change-capable workforce.

While a good blueprint is necessary for a great outcome, it is not sufficient to create one. The principles must be applied with the glue of authentic leadership. Without the appropriate glue the carefully assembled principles will not hold together. When the principles are applied correctly, the resulting emergent properties will happily surprise even the most optimistic change leader.

When the twelve principles are followed, change happens more quickly and effectively. With each successive change, competency and capability are increased and we get better at seeing the opportunities in change. With the principles of **Making Change Stick**, embracing change becomes a reality rather than a pipe dream. Change-capable or change-paralyzed, the choice is ours.

I hear that Sisyphus is looking for a new assignment!

When we see the need for deep change, we usually see it as something that needs to take place in someone else. In our roles of authority, such as parent, teacher, or boss, we are particularly quick to direct others to change. Such directives often fail, and we respond to the resistance by increasing our efforts. The power struggle that follows seldom results in change or brings about excellence. One of the most important insights about the need to bring about deep change in others has to do with where deep change actually starts.

~ Robert E. Quinn

Making Change Stick

Acknowledgments

LITTLE of substance can be created without the help and advice of others. Had it not been for the encouragement of those around me, the decades of lip-flapping about writing a book would likely have continued without tangible outcome. Let me first thank those who saw in me what I could not see in myself—in particular two wonderful leaders, Joe Burd and Dick Walker, who were instrumental in helping me hone my leadership skills early in my career. I am thankful for the many colleagues and clients who have shared their time, thoughts, and experiences as we learned together.

Thanks to my colleague Janet Werner for introducing me to the Bridges change model and for the many hours of thoughtful dialogue about vision, leadership, and change. I also wish to thank Bruce Emra, Diane Ferrara, Mike Ghizzone, Stan Janosz, Lisa Peterson, Robert Reale, and Neal Strohmeyer who read and commented on earlier drafts of the book. Special thanks to Neal Strohmeyer for being a constant source of positive support and having the faith to open up his company as a learning laboratory over the last twelve years.

Thanks to Ken Smith for keeping the computer systems running and creating those dandy chapter numbers and cover. Finally, I am deeply indebted to my dear friend and editor, Ellen Van Landingham, who hacked my dangling participles, unmixed my metaphors, disposed of superfluous words, and held my feet to the fire to make this book a reality. I thank God for these good people and for the grace that has helped me grow rather than wither through my own difficult transitions.

References

1. Crosby, Philip B. *Quality Is Free: the Art of Making Quality Certain*. McGraw-Hill, 1979.

2. Conner, Daryl. *Managing At The Speed Of Change: How Resilient Managers Succeed and Prosper Where Others Fail*. Villard Books, 1993.

3. Bridges, William. *Transitions: Making Sense of Life's Changes*. Addison-Wesley, 1980.

4. Kubler-Ross, Elisabeth. *On Death And Dying*. Macmillan, 1969.

5. Marston, William Moulton. *Emotions of Normal People*. Harcourt, Brace and Company, 1928.

6. Bonnstetter, Bill J. and Judy I. Suiter. *The Universal Language DISC: A Reference Manual*. Target Training International, Ltd., 2004.

7. Newberg, Andrew B., Eugene G. d'Aquili, and Vince Rause. *Why God Won't Go Away: Brain Science and the Biology of Belief*. Ballantine Books, 2001.

8. Collins, Jim. *Good To Great: Why Some Companies Make the Leap – And Others Don't*. HarperBusiness, 2001.

9. Goleman, Daniel. *Emotional Intelligence*. Bantam Books, 1995.

10. Gladwell, Malcolm. *The Tipping Point: How Little Things Can Make A Big Difference*. Little, Brown, 2000.

Index

About The Author

RICHARD REALE earned his Bachelor of Engineering and Master of Science degrees from Stevens Institute of Technology. He has held key leadership positions in organizations ranging from start-up companies to Fortune 500 corporations and has taught Organizational Behavior at Ramapo College of New Jersey.

With a long track record of implementing systemic change, Rich established Positive Impact Associates in 1993 to help create environments that foster performance excellence. His methods combine traditional and leading-edge philosophies to enhance individual performance and group collaboration.